Juan Pablo
Montoya

Other books by **Christopher Hilton**

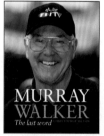

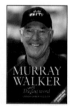

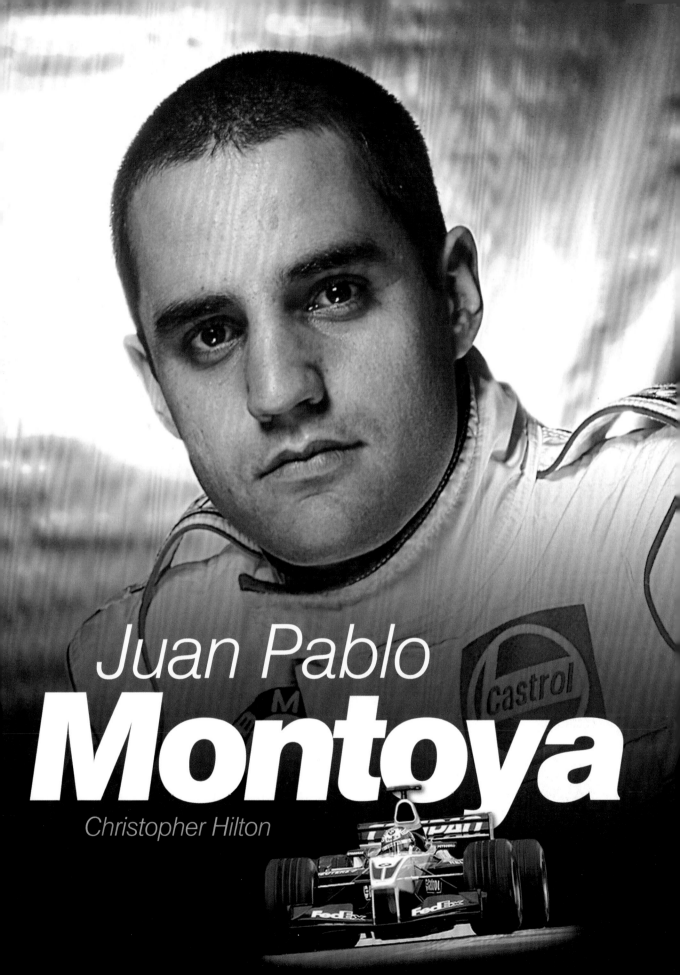

Juan Pablo
Montoya

Christopher Hilton

(Getty Images)

First published in March 2003

A catalogue record for this book is available from the British Library

ISBN 1 85960 998 8

Library of Congress catalog card no 2002 117293

Haynes North America Inc., 861 Lawrence Drive, Newbury Park, California 91320, USA.

Published by Haynes Publishing, Sparkford, Yeovil, Somerset BA22 7JJ, UK.

Tel: 01963 442030 Fax: 01963 440001
Int.tel: +44 1963 442030 Int.fax: +44 1963 440001
E-mail: sales@haynes-manuals.co.uk
Website: www.haynes.co.uk

Designed by Simon Larkin
Printed and bound in Britain by
J. H. Haynes & Co. Ltd, Sparkford

contents

The foundation of Montoya's career was always solid because father and son were so close. Pablo gave up his own racing to concentrate on Juan Pablo's – in the early years, karting consumed most weekends. (Getty Images)

the monster mash
introduction

'There's an expression in the United States *someone's got iced water in their veins* and that's how he drives: take no prisoners, don't give a damn, don't be intimidated by anybody or anything. He was no more intimidated by Michael Andretti than he was by Michael Schumacher…'

The speaker is Robin Miller, based at Indianapolis, the hub of United States motorsport. He's been writing about racing for more than three decades and keeps a knowing eye on both sides of the Atlantic. He's speaking about Juan Pablo Montoya who represents important, perhaps crucial, aspects of Grand Prix racing's future.

Who is this Montoya? A clue comes in the driver's own words, echoing Miller's perception. 'I can't be bothering about what other drivers think.'

What are your strengths?

'My self-confidence and the ability to adjust to new circuits fairly quickly.'

Do you have any weaknesses?

'I don't know.'

What has been your worst experience so far?

'I haven't had any bad experiences.'

What about being famous?

'Fame means nothing. The only thing you can say about fame is that it makes your life a lot more difficult than it is already.'

Further clues in Montoya's racing career suggest that he is both mentally and physically able to mount a serious challenge to Schumacher, whose dominance – with Ferrari – was so complete that for the 2003 season there were even absurd murmurings of handicaps. In 2002 Schumacher won 11 races and his team-mate Rubens Barrichello four. Ferrari were in a position to decide which one would win (and did so in Austria), and the drivers themselves were so far in front they could indulge themselves for their own amusement. At Indianapolis at the end of the US Grand Prix, evidently, they tried to stage a dead heat.

No ordinary driver could expect to break this dominance. But Montoya might.

Montoya takes pole at Monza in 2001 – a year later he would drive the fastest ever Formula 1 lap there. (LAT)

The first clue to this came in the CART series during qualifying at his début race on an oval circuit: Motegi, Japan. He was driving for the Chip Ganassi team, with Mo Nunn as his engineer. Montoya happened to be on a flying lap at the same time as Michael Andretti, who had been racing this formula since *1983*, was out on the track. They reached Turn Three.

'Juan thought Michael did a brake job to unnerve him,' Nunn says, 'and when they came down the front straight Juan went up the side of him and started doing *this* [squeezing gesture] – no contact – and then he accelerated and actually misjudged it. He went to go in front of Michael and then turn into the corner, and they touched, but Michael was against the wall and couldn't do anything. They were 190mph. So they both crash into the wall, Juan gets out to go and see if Michael's OK. He runs over and Michael has got out of the car and he's screaming. He's calling him an effing idiot and "you're trying to

effing kill me". Juan's never had the experience of a driver reacting like that in an accident. He started to laugh and Michael took it *really* bad.'

The second clue came in 2001 when Montoya reached Formula 1: Brazil, third race of the season. He overtook Michael Schumacher for the lead in the corkscrew left–right at the end of the straight with a move so daring that, within an eyeblink, a new power had arrived in Grand Prix.

The third clue came at the 2001 Italian Grand Prix. 'People often talk about Interlagos because it concerned Michael,' Montoya will say, 'but there was also Monza where I had to pass him if I wanted to win the race. The team told me by radio *you must pass Michael.* I did it, because you never know how much fuel the bloke in front has. To wait for your opponent to refuel is to take too big a risk. Me, I prefer to overtake him because I am there to run. An overtaking move is difficult and easy all at the same time. You

have to decide to go or not. It's as simple as that.'

There's a different kind of clue, centred on self-discipline and driver conduct.

'We drove together for a couple of years in the States,' Mark Blundell says, 'and I've been side-by-side at 230mph with him. When you do that you have to know and trust the other guy. That's a mutual respect thing because you are in each other's hands. There were some guys that you had to think twice about but at the Montoya level no, not a problem.

'He has awesome car control, doesn't have any sort of respect for anybody in terms of what they may have achieved or what their credentials are. As far as he's concerned, on the race circuit it's dog eat dog. Montoya and Andretti had to play each other out, and Montoya's way of doing that was to stand his ground. Then we saw Montoya do that with Schumacher. Same deal. That's Montoya stating his case: *no-one's going to shove me about*.'

. . . and how to concentrate. Montoya-power at Monaco, 2001 – clean, pure and immense. (Getty Images)

In an era where so many young couples live together, Montoya and Connie went the more old fashioned route – and invited 400 guests to Colombia to celebrate their marriage. (AFP)

And talking of car control, in 1995 Nigel Mihell – fresh out of karts and intending to be the first black Formula 1 driver – saw Montoya walking round the garage at Mallory Park, 'Latin guy, very purposeful'. Mihell ventured out in an old 2-litre car and decided to follow the Latin guy, who was with Paul Stewart Racing. Mihell stayed with him until a corner. Then 'what was killing me in the head was that the back of his car was sliding out as it pulled away. The back was at such an angle that I could see his nearside front wheel! I watched him opposite-locking the car all the way round and still pull away.' When Mihell got back the team said *don't mark yourself against him, he's something else.* He is indeed.

But beating Schumacher for a championship?

'There's a huge amount of ability and he has a huge future but probably he still needs to prove that he's complete, he's rounded enough to get the job done in the overall scheme of things. If it went on ability and car control alone, he'd win hands down. As a bloke he was fine, very pleasant, very open, good with my kids – the boys – very amicable guy.'

That's the other Montoya. Bob Dance, once a central member of the Lotus Grand Prix team and latterly working for a Formula 3 team called Tom's, saw it too. In 1997 they were running an Argentinian, Brian Smith. Montoya had progressed to Formula 3000 so 'they weren't driving together but Montoya was his mate – they used to have a lot of fun and we saw a bit more of him than the others. I thought he was a proper racer. I liked him and still do. I don't think he's over-complicated, he just gets on with the job and he's got some balls. He is big enough not to clutter his head with things that don't matter. If you give him an equal chance with Michael Schumacher he won't back off. Senna wasn't a man to back off, was he?'

Any comparisons with Ayrton Senna are perhaps questionable, but several people make them during the course of this book.

I do not want, incidentally, to be distracted by qualifying at the 2002 Italian Grand Prix when Montoya took the Williams-BMW round at an average speed of 161.449mph, the fastest Formula 1 lap ever driven. [The engine was delivering 19,050rpm, another first.] The lap represented a consummation of what a driver can make a fast car do.

Montoya has what Frank Williams describes as the 'gladiator' in him and, after the overtaking move at Interlagos the Williams crew were calling him The Monster. In the context of Formula 1 this is a very great compliment. Apart from Jacques Villeneuve – who'd done a bit of monstering in his time – and Eddie Irvine, the other drivers tended to be clean cut, verbally prudent and forever beige.

Montoya was the antidote. He spoke as curtly or expansively as he wanted and if you didn't like it, tough. He had charisma beyond what you'd anticipate from a tanned, macho man. He had a wonderful way of conjuring sunshine when he smiled. He had the eyes of a naughty kid, full of delights and, right from the beginning – in karts in his native Colombia, when he *was* a kid – he had something.

This book is about how the something grew first in Europe, then in the United States, then in Europe again. I've tried to include a description of as many of Montoya's races as possible to chart his progress.

I'm indebted to many good people who have helped with memories, background and factual information. I list them in no particular order: Jonny and Lesley-Ann Kane; Paul Stewart; Declan Betts; Robin Miller of ESPN; Victor G. Ricardo, Colombian Ambassador in London, and the Cultural Attaché, Carlos Eduardo Osorio – and Rosemary Helfer, who translated with consummate skill; Richard Dutton of Fortec; Nate Siebens of CART; Barry Waddell; Vic Elford; Peter Dumbreck; Andrew Warres of the Skip Barber School; Rod MacLeod; Morris Nunn; Natt Pendleton of the Indianapolis Motor Speedway; Ron Green of the IRL; Patrick of the Monaco Press Office; Bruce Grant-Braham for sending photographs and giving a delightful interview; Peter Walker of BMW Special Events; Michael Andretti; Carol Wilkins and Tom McGovern of Team Green; Formula 3000 team-mate Gareth Rees; Marcus Pye; Greg Ray and his indefatigable PR Kathy Prather; Agnes Carlier and Nick Heidfeld of Sauber; Bill Janitz, Public Relations Manager of Michigan International Speedway; Bob Dance, formerly of Lotus and now with Tom's; Mark Blundell; David Sears of Super Nova.

Michael Easterbrook, a freelance journalist, conducted invaluable interviews in Bogotá with Jose Clopatofsky, Elmer Vega and Enrique Leal. 'Clopa' sent pictures and advised on facts. Juan Vega also supplied photographs.

I pay my respects to various sources which have been helpful. *Formula 1* magazine has interviewed Montoya repeatedly and in interesting ways; *Autosport* is unrivalled in the depth of its coverage; while the *Auto course* annuals and the *Marlboro Grand Prix Guide* were never far from my elbow. I have also leaned heavily on the 2000 *Daily Trackside Report* produced by Indianapolis Motor Speedway.

The attitude the world would come to know: laid back, and with the broadest of smiles. (Getty Images)

internal force

Colombia is a country we tend to know for all the wrong reasons, because we see it in terms of newspaper headlines and television bulletins about the drug trafficking, civil war, kidnappings and murders. Colombia is, of course, only fractionally this and the ordinary inhabitants living their peaceful everyday lives are complete strangers to us. Few Westerners could name any Colombian other than Juan Pablo Montoya.

'There are many characteristic features of our culture,' says the Colombian Cultural Attaché in London, Carlos Eduardo Osorio. 'What happened at the time of the discovery of Colombia left its mark on the future. Colombia had an indigenous population with a very specific hierarchical structure. Then the Spaniards arrived [in the capital Bogotá in 1535] and said "we have discovered you! From now on all these lands belong to the king of Spain."

'Many of the permanent social phenomena have arrived because of invasions. It exists in the form of a collective memory which has made the Colombian character have a certain amount of internal aggression. Colombians would be much more aggressive if it wasn't for the Catholic education which has softened a lot of the instincts.

'The population is a mixture of the Spanish, the indigenous people and the Africans who came as slaves. Inside Colombian people there is a certain tenacity, a determination, a strength which belongs to those whose pride has been touched: an internal force which makes Colombians do something risky and daring. *That* is part of Colombian culture.'[1]

It is also a very interesting observation to make about a racing driver.

When Colombians look at Montoya, do they see themselves?

'Yes. Juan Pablo mirrors the Colombian prototype.'

This is emphasised by Montoya's love of his country – '*my* country, *my* home. It means a lot to me. It's a great place and I really enjoy being there. I love the food, the people, everything.'

After the 2002 season he went back there to marry his Colombian fiancée Connie, a law graduate from Madrid. The country evidently surrendered to Montoya and he needed three bodyguards: not to prevent kidnapping but to keep him from being physically overwhelmed by well-wishers.

Montoya understands what he means to his country. 'In Colombia I like to present a good image to the children. Kids look at me and I'm something they want to get to be.'

After a visit in 2001 he said[2] 'I couldn't believe my eyes! I can excite enough desire for people there to get up at six in the morning on a Sunday to watch the races. It's fantastic. Me, I used to do that when I was a kid because I was always crazy about Formula 1 but, at that time, it was not a very popular sport in Colombia. Now people are fans of it and I'm happy that it's a little bit because of me. They have breakfast among friends in front of the television. That's nice – because it's real life!'

Osorio says: 'People ask each other "where are you going to watch the race? Shall we get together at so-and-so?" Whole families watch them.'

The way we were:
the Boy Scouts'
graduation
ceremony,
Bogotá, 1985.
(Jose Clopatofsky)

Starting at the very
top – in karts.
(courtesy El Tiempo)

(Note: To avoid any confusion between Pablo and Juan Pablo in this chapter, I call the father Pablo and the son Montoya.)

Colombia, independent from Spain since 1819, is in the north west of South America. It's a poor country of tropical rainforests, uplands and mountains: not promising terrain for motorsport, you'd think, although in discussing how difficult it was for a Colombian to make it Montoya has said: 'It is the same wherever you are from. I was lucky enough because when I needed the money it was there, and I always had the backing. I think wherever you are from it's difficult, though – in England there are too many drivers and not enough sponsors. I was the only driver from Colombia and there was not much sponsorship either but we always managed to get support.'

Bogotá, 2,640 metres above sea level, has a population of eight million. Like most major cities worldwide, its architecture mingles modern buildings with earlier influences, in this case dating back to the Spanish colonial times. The country's troubles happen largely elsewhere. Furthermore, as Osorio points out, 'people around the world think Colombia is experiencing a civil war. The reality is that Colombia has 42 million inhabitants and the world thinks 21 million are fighting the other 21 million. It's not like that. The most the guerrillas have is 30,000 people. The rest are people who work to live.'

Montoya's grandfather Santiago worked in real estate as well as building houses. He was successful enough to be one of the first to have a holiday home on the Caribbean island of San Andres, belonging to Colombia. Santiago's wife Sofia was the one who did the driving – on the roads – taking the family on trips in an orange VW Beetle of an early 1960s vintage. Maybe it all started there.

Colombia's first racetrack was built privately by a wealthy man called Ricardo Mejia, not far from the centre of Bogotá. To inaugurate this, in 1971, he invited leading European drivers to compete in a couple of Formula 2 races over consecutive weekends. (Between the races some drivers went to have a look at the jungle; others headed up to the Caribbean.) Twenty drivers took part, including Graham Hill in a works Lotus, Rolf Stommelen, Jo Siffert and Henri Pescarolo. The races were won by Siffert and Alan Rollinson. Pescarolo was the number one in a March team being run by a certain Frank Williams. It so happened that Williams was standing outside the Hotel Tequendama in the city centre and noticed an Olivetti advertising hoarding across the main street. Hmm, he thought. He went to Olivetti and raised $5,000 sponsorship.

Jose Clopatofsky, former sports editor of the leading newspaper *El Tiempo*, covered the races and also competed in a race for locals after the Formula 2s. He had a Wartburg, an East German product 'with a very ugly aluminium body made by myself. I won with this curious machine and made a huge impression. I have pictures of Hill and Siffert looking at it.' He was invited to race in Europe, did and ran out of money.

Back in Colombia 'I created with friends of my age a club named Escuderia Tres Cilindros because most of us had DKWs and Wartburgs[3]. Among the founders was Pablo Montoya. Many meetings were held at his house and we usually did some laps around the block. It was a residential area and the neighbours would call the police to protest about the night races round their houses. Pablo had a Wartburg and did some races but wasn't very successful. The car had many mechanical problems and was parked outside his house. It stayed there until a passer-by saw it and offered Pablo's wife

Libia some money for it. She immediately accepted and bought a vacuum cleaner with the money.' This was in 1972, the year of their marriage. Clopatofsky also talks discreetly of other 'illegal' races on some nights which he, his wife, Pablo and Libia attended before retreating (or advancing) to the discos nearby. Pablo was never seen to dance. It cannot have been because he lacked natural balance as he was an accomplished roller skater and even took part in long-distance races. The love of skating was something Montoya would inherit.

Libia (née Roldan) is known for being quiet and, although she followed the races, never showed much emotion, preferring to be in the background. She is evidently an expert cook.

On 20 September 1975, Juan Pablo Montoya was

Début in single-seaters: Formula Colombia cars – which were Van Diemens with Renault engines. (courtesy El Tiempo)

A delightful study of Montoya and Jaime Guerrero. Montoya would watch Jaime's brother Roberto in Formula 1 from afar. (courtesy El Tiempo)

born in Bogotá. It would be a full family, with a brother – Federico – and sisters Liliana and Katalina. It was also a middle class family: dad was an architect. They represented, Osorio says, 'a traditional family. They have a modest car, the habit of going out as a family and playing sport. They don't have extra money to spare. Colombia is a poor country: over 50% live in poverty and there is a big gap between the rich and the poor. People who attend motor races do not belong to the poorer classes.' Paradoxically, Osorio adds that 'Colombians don't normally travel much because, I think, of the family system. They are very inward looking.'

Not the Montoyas. Liliana, now married with two children, used to race karts against the boys – and Montoya. She was good, only stopping when she became pregnant. Katalina studies psychology in Miami. She raced karts and competed in the Renault Twingo Cup where she was a finalist against Clopatofsky's son. Montoya was there and 'prepared her with great care, spending a lot of time on the track with her'. Federico, who is close to Montoya, now races karts in Miami although he wasn't keen until a couple of years ago. Pablo says Federico was somewhat intimidated by the name and pressure of being Montoya's brother but Montoya pushed him and he competes now too.

The Montoya family lived in San Jose de Bavaria, a neighbourhood – then under construction – of big houses with sprawling gardens, protected by stone walls, along uncrowded, peaceful streets. The house itself was a decent size: a red-tiled roof, trees, well kept; nice but not gaudy. Montoya was educated at Colegio Gimnasio Bilingüe Campestre and later Colegio San Tarcisio, both private schools.

To picture the young Montoya, here are three people who knew him then.

Clopatofsky is editor of *Motor*, a car magazine published twice a month with *El Tiempo*. He's the second cousin of Pablo and has known Montoya since birth. Clopatofsky says Montoya was a normal lad – in the Boy Scouts, for instance – but not easily intimidated. He was courageous, confident, with a strong mind, and 'always had good direction from his father'.

Enrique Leal, a long-time friend of Pablo, would become Montoya's mechanic and helper at the track. He describes Montoya as very affectionate as a kid but also very rebellious. 'He always insisted on getting whatever he wanted.'

Elmer Vega's son Angelo would become a leading competitor with Montoya. Elmer has known Montoya since he was six and describes him as playful, hyperactive, happy, very daring and extroverted: a good friend.

When Montoya was five, Pablo taught him how to drive, sitting the boy on his knee. All are agreed that, virtually from the beginning, Montoya was good. All are also agreed that Pablo saw this potential, and managed it with great skill. As Vega puts it, Montoya had 'special talents and always wanted to race'; Clopatofsky says Pablo's dream was for Montoya to become a famous driver.

As the fledgeling career got more serious the Montoyas would be a familiar presence at the Kartodromo Cajicá, a track some 20 minutes drive from Bogotá. It was the first in Colombia and, until then, karters had had to use the streets or parking lots. In 1980 Pablo designed the circuit, got financial backing for this and led an effort to create a junior category, which began in 1983 and had about ten races a year. The number of drivers varied from around 12 to as many as 27. It must have been a good proving ground for Montoya.

By this time, Montoya's uncle Diego was competing at a high level of motorsport. Clopatofsky says Diego was a 'big, big driver who also had a strong influence on Montoya's career. He was in CanAm and IMSA.' He drove a Sauber BMW at Le Mans in 1983 as one of a three-man team 'with Tony Garcia and Alberto Naon, Cuban guys that lived in Miami'. Clopatofsky remembers that Sauber didn't have a wind tunnel in those days and was concerned about the car's stability on the long Mulsanne straight. The team put a pointer in the cockpit – linked to the suspension arms – which would show the car's ride height and what it was doing aerodynamically. Diego went out first and hadn't been round Le Mans before. He did an installation lap and Sauber asked about the pointer. Diego had hardly noticed it, went out again and watched. He reported

Sir Frank Williams went to the Chicago CART race in 2000, and listened carefully. (Getty Images)

that the pointer was to the extreme right, 'meaning that the nose was very high and the front wheels lifting'. Sauber changed the car and had a new nose put on it: Diego and Co. finished ninth. *Autosport* wrote that 'the first non-Porsche home was the pretty Sauber, a model of reliability ... during the consistent pilotage of Garcia/Naon, Montoia' [sic].

By this time, young Montoya had fallen for Grand Prix racing as well as karting. A Colombian, Roberto Guerrero, reached Formula 1 in 1982 with a team called Ensign Racing and, for 1983, moved to Theodore Racing. 'I watched him most of the time. I used to be a big fan of his when I was a little kid.' Later Montoya followed Ayrton Senna's career, which would provide 'some of my earliest memories'. Senna became a hero.

Montoya's own career became more serious in 1984 when he won the junior category. All agree that Pablo was the central figure. Montoya himself explains that 'my dad was very patient and never pushed me. You might call him the ideal racing dad. I owe everything to him. Since I started racing, he supported me in everything: economically, mentally and physically. He took me to all the races, no matter how far from home.'

On the matter of expense, Osorio says 'his father mortgaged the house in order for Juan Pablo's racing career. Very often in Colombia the father stakes all for his son.' This did not happen until Montoya reached Formula 3000 in Europe, his enormous potential was established and the big bills started to come in.

Clopatofsky coins a lovely phrase. 'To make a jewel it takes a long time. I think Pablo deserves all the credit.'

Harmony, however, could be elusive.

Clopatofsky explains that Pablo 'never made things easy' for Montoya. He'd have him start at the back of races to practise passing, or driving a kart which wasn't the best to make the races more challenging, but he took care to encourage him whenever he lost. In fact, Pablo worked a lot with Montoya on passing, and evolved a tactic (much used by Senna) of forcing the kart hard immediately – when the other drivers would be just settling – even though the tyres were cold. 'He has always been very aggressive at the beginning of races.' In sum, Montoya had real speed and didn't crash very often. 'He was better than all of them but once in a while he lost.'

Leal confirms that Pablo frequently powered down the motor and inhibited the kart in other ways to hone the lad's skill. Montoya didn't always appreciate that. 'He would finish some races crying and angry.' Leal adds that one of Montoya's greatest talents was knowing his kart well and having a good sense of it on the track: when to accelerate, *how* to accelerate out of the corners. 'He didn't do it for fun. He took it very professionally.' Leal is sure Pablo has been crucial to Montoya's success: the two loved each other but also clashed quite a bit. 'It was always a difficult relationship. Both are very stubborn.'

Vega explains that Montoya used to get angry with

Pablo because – another tactic, to make the boy mechanically literate? – he didn't help prepare the kart. Montoya 'screamed and yelled at his dad' about that. This happened during the first three years as a kart racer – but, in fact, Montoya was interested in the mechanics of the kart. His character was strong, he was an aggressive young racer and 'he always wanted to win'. When he did lose he became angry. He was, however, a gracious winner.

Racing consumed most Montoya weekends. They'd compete at eight tracks throughout Colombia but mainly at Cajicá. Montoya went there between three and six times a month, and showed tremendous enthusiasm.

He became one of the top karters in the country, winning championships and even competing (until 1994) as an overlap to his car racing. Pablo gave up his own racing to concentrate on his son's. As Clopatofsky says, Pablo 'spent a lot of money to keep him racing'.

Rod MacLeod, who met the Montoyas when Juan Pablo was driving in Mexico, says 'the way that he went about his racing had a lot to do with his father's influence. I think his father is a very intense person – the times I've seen him with Juan Pablo it's always been like that. I've witnessed both sides of the father, the side where he is very splendid and you can see him helping young karting guys from Colombia, and the side where he can be a bit of a hard nut: strict, difficult to please, someone that could be very, very intense especially as far as the races are concerned. You can see where Juan Pablo got that from.'

This must be contrasted with the words of Morris Nunn,[4] who'd be Montoya's race engineer in the United States in 1999. 'Dad is a super guy, doesn't put pressure on his son like some fathers do. A very nice person, the whole family are, and never really interfered. Very proud of his son and wants him to go further.'

Inevitably, Pablo's racing career has been lost in the shadows of what Montoya has achieved but here is a glimpse of it. Circa 1986, Pablo took part in a karting championship in Neiva, south of Bogotá, and among others beat a Brazilian teenager called Rubens Barrichello. When Montoya won his first Grand Prix, the Italian in 2001, he beat this same Barrichello by 5.175 seconds…

Montoya first drove a car at 14. It was a decisive moment. At that point, Osorio reports, 'motor racing was not important in Colombia'. Previous drivers had 'aroused people's interest but didn't make them really passionate about it'.

Football was the big sport. Cycling was also popular but the country hasn't had a good cyclist in years. Montoya has replaced it and, anyway, Colombians are attracted by the risks in motor racing.

'There are a few Colombians who reach great heights,' Osorio says, 'and to a certain extent they reflect the longings of the 42 million other Colombians. They'd love to achieve the same if they had the opportunity – but for many Colombians, life is a matter of survival.'

So is motor racing, and Juan Pablo Montoya fully intended to explore that. He became almost an antidote to Colombia's problems. Jose Clopatofsky expresses it beautifully. 'He's Latin, he's explosive, and he's bloody quick. He's a positive ambassador, the whole country is inside his car when he's racing and the show is only just beginning.'

NOTES

1. There's a laid-back aspect to the Colombian character too, as Mr Osorio suggests in this joke. A man went to hell and the Devil asked which version he wanted: the English, the Russian or the Colombian? The man wondered how to choose and the Devil said 'let's look.' The English: at *exactly* 6am someone comes to light the computerised ovens and at *exactly* 6pm he changes it into ice. The Russian: a comrade arrives *about* 6am to light the gas ovens and *about* 6pm switches it to ice. The Colombian: the ovens burn wood but *sometimes* there isn't any and *sometimes* no oil to fuel them either; *sometimes* the man doesn't turn up, *sometimes* he does but forgets his matches, and *sometimes* he'd been kidnapped. The inmates spend their time playing cards…

2. *AUTOhebdo*, a French motoring magazine.

3. Escuderia Tres Cilindros, Three Cylinder Club. DKW were part of Audi. Wartburgs were, to an East German, upmarket saloons.

4. As Clopatofsky points out, by a 'curious coincidence' Nunn was also Guerrero's manager in Formula 1 as owner of Ensign. 'Colombians always sustain connections.'

Right from the early days, the importance of good preparation was instilled into Montoya - but there would never be much need for advice on charisma. (Getty Images)

body language

'I was the lead instructor for a Skip Barber Racing School at Sears Point[1] in 1992,' Vic Elford will say, his voice as English as the day he left to live in the United States these many years ago. 'It was around about July, August, he'd just turned 17 and he arrived for the School. I didn't know him from Adam. He hadn't driven a racing car before, I think. It had all been karting.'

Montoya was about to take the step from karts to cars. There comes a moment where the ambitious driver must decide if motor racing could be his career, and a professional driving school like Skip Barber will help to inform the decision.

Elford, a Londoner, had driven in Grands Prix in the 1960s and then in sports cars but, more than that, he understood the psychology of teaching.

'Juan Pablo came with his dad and did not speak one word of English. I can speak a little Spanish but certainly not enough to teach people in it. Dad spoke quite good English. I was the one directly in contact with Juan Pablo and I had to do all the translating through the dad.'

Elford gives a comparison to show how instinctively good Montoya was – already.

We had another student in the class, Jeff Bucknum, son of Ronnie.[2] He was quite good, terribly enthusiastic and with a huge will to win, but he just didn't have the laid-back, calm, reflective intuition that Montoya had. Montoya just sat, listened, and then did exactly what we told him to do. Exactly. Everything, every single time.

It's a three-day course using – then – Formula Ford 1600s. On day one, the first thing they had was a little slalom exercise weaving in and out of five cones, followed by a "straight line" exercise with the cones: we told them to go through in second gear at 2,000rpm, no on and off the throttle, keep it steady. After that, we put the speed up a little bit and had them repeat it two or three times.

Then we had them doing the same thing but once they'd got past the first cone they must gently squeeze the throttle so that they accelerated all the way through. It was up to their judgement – although they had to do it so that at no time did they lift off. In other words, they decided how much they squeezed, when and where. The idea was to keep accelerating and most people can't do it because it's not easy at all: most either accelerate too much – which means that at some point they have to lift – or they don't quite accelerate enough.

Having done that we tell them "OK, as you're coming around the third cone, the one in the middle, we want you to be accelerating absolutely flat out. Once the car is halfway round that cone – the front wheels are turning, the car is turning – at that point simply snap off the throttle. And when you do that, what's going to happen? The back of the car is going to step out and you learn the first basic rule: if you get to the stage where you know you're going to spin, use both feet – left foot in on the clutch to keep the engine running, right foot hard on the brake to lock everything up. That's the

surest and safest way to stop. We don't want you to do that. We want you to snap off the throttle. Obviously the back's going to come around and now it's both feet out of the pedals. Don't even think about going near the throttle or the clutch. From now on you recover simply with the steering wheel, and you do that by instantly turning in to the skid, stabilising it and then, once the car is under control, slowly bring the wheel back straight. Then you drive on again…

During the course of the three days they'll be learning about braking, because braking isn't just sticking your foot on the pedal. There's a lot more to it than that. As the course gets further on we'll talk about overtaking, how it's done, how you work up to it and that sort of thing. We'll talk about starting a race. For example, one of the philosophies I developed on my own as part of my teaching – others didn't do it – was asking the young drivers about being on the grid but not being on the front row. "Let's say you're on the second or third row. What psychologically is the most difficult thing to do when you are waiting for the start? You have to convince yourself the guy in front is going to get away perfectly because if you don't you won't. If you're waiting to see what he does, one thing is absolutely obvious: you've lost out."

Anyway, the course goes along very slowly and carefully, starting with low revs and building them up – and building up the speed. Out on the circuit, as the revs build, the gears for each corner change but the drivers are always very restricted. One of the very few people I have ever seen who could relate to those restrictions and still do a perfect job was Montoya. If we said "2,700rpm" that's what he did, if we said "4,000rpm" that's what he did.

Until midday on the third day, they are only doing a lap at a time and there's no overtaking anywhere. Then the mechanics on the start-finish line hand them an onboard radio so the instructors all around the circuit can give feedback, corner by corner, if they feel the drivers need it. After that they are sent off for a couple of sessions of about 20 minutes each where they are doing continual laps. They'd probably be doing ten laps the first time and a dozen the second.

Clearly they are not all going to be at the same speed so overtaking is permitted, but again this is very controlled. It is only permitted on specific parts on any one track, which [in effect] means the straight, and before a guy can go by he has to

receive a hand signal from the driver in front, a hand saying "yes, you can overtake". They are only allowed to overtake then, and only on the right. Otherwise it could get very dangerous.

Let's take Sears Point specifically. By this time they're up to using maximum 5,000rpm in whatever gear they're in. For a race weekend the rev limit on those cars would be set at 6,000 and they couldn't go over it, but at the School we didn't play with the rev limiter. The drivers were just told 5,000rpm.

Montoya was unbelievable. Other instructors were saying to me "look at X, you can see he's trying" and indeed you could, he was trying very hard and he wasn't respecting 5,000rpm. Montoya on the other hand was respecting it – and we checked the rev counters afterwards, but you can hear it anyway. After a while, you know what these cars are doing.

While he was going through the course there were plenty of other drivers around because, typically, 14 to 16 pupils are involved. There was a direct comparison when we got to the unrestricted part – in fact even before that – and it became very obvious that although Montoya didn't seem to be bothered by what he was being asked to do, others were. In fact one was clearly very bothered trying to

show he was going to be at least as good as Montoya, whereas Montoya didn't need to prove that. It was a bit Senna-esque. "I am the best because I know I am." That's how I felt he felt, and that's how I felt about him. Incidentally, we rapidly made sure they were separated on the track, just in case…

Montoya was rigidly respecting the 5,000rpm, he was clean, beautiful, and fast everywhere. In fact, at Sears Point – which is not the easiest track in the world – he was only two or three seconds off the outright lap record by the end of the afternoon, and of course he was only using the 5,000 whilst the record for those cars was set using 6,000. He could get that close because he was so good at everything he was doing, braking and cornering. You can only teach people so much of this: it is something you are born with.

As an instructor I used to say I could teach anybody who turned up at the Skip Barber Racing School to be a good driver but I couldn't teach anybody to be a great driver. It comes from within, and that's exactly how I felt with him. I think I taught him a lot, and I am sure he learned a lot, but after that it came from himself.

When we'd finished the School I announced to all the other instructors: "You know, you guys are really

JUAN PABLO MONTOYA BODY LANGUAGE

The ex-karters Montoya and Angelo Vega keep in touch with a night on the town! (Juan Vega)

The ex-karters Montoya and Angelo Vega keep in touch with a night on the town! (Juan Vega)

Brothers in arms. From the left, Federico Montoya, dad, friends Jorge Sarmiento and Juan Gabriel Lopez, Montoya, Angelo, Jaime Guerrero. (Juan Vega)

lucky. We've just been teaching a future World Champion." I absolutely felt it as strongly as that. I took his dad to one side and said "don't tell Juan Pablo, but he's going to be World Champion." With all the teaching I've done over the years I have never ever taught anyone who came even remotely close to him.

Juan Pablo struck me as a wonderful bloke. He has obviously changed physically now – it's a little bit like Antonio Pizzonia.[3] When I first knew Antonio he was a scraggly, skinny little kid and now he's grown into an attractive young man. Montoya was the same at 17.

I'll tell you another thing about Montoya. I presume he had come to the School in preparation for Formula Renault in Colombia, to find out how you did it before he got into a car race. That formula was small racing cars, all with Renault engines, similar to Formula Ford 2000.[4]

He went back to Colombia from the School and his very first race was a couple of weeks afterwards – in Formula Renault. There were some pretty good drivers down there and his dad sent me a tape: Juan Pablo was fastest in practice and led three quarters of the race but he knew nothing about tyre management or any of that sort of thing. Towards the end he

was being challenged very hard by one of the veterans. As they came down into a fairly tight right-hander the veteran had obviously summoned up all his courage and said to himself this is where I am going to overtake. He was very late on the brakes. Montoya had glanced in the mirror, seen him coming and sat there until he'd gone by then drove inside, re-took him and went off again.

Thereby hangs a tale. An experienced driver, David Sears, watched this race and it would have a profound significance deep into Montoya's future. 'I was doing the Bogotá six-hour race because I used to race in Formula 3 with Roberto Guerrero and a friend of his invited me. People came from all over South America to do it. There were 58 cars – I was in a CanAm car. Montoya was doing his first car race, Formula Renault, after karts where he'd been very successful. He was on pole by half a mile and although it was only a ten or twelve lap race he won it by half a lap so obviously I thought he was a man to watch.' Sears would do that.

Elford explains that Montoya also did some touring cars when he went back. 'I think his dad told me in total that year he drove in 19 races and won 14 of them. Elford has the most vivid recollection of the 'Senna-esque' side to Montoya. Barber were running a series with Saabs and Montoya intended to compete in it. 'He did his first Barber Saab race in 1993 – a one-off at Mid-Ohio – to have a look at it all before he drove the whole 1994 season.' In Barber Saab he'd be competing against – among others – Barry Waddell, later a coach at Barber. Waddell says:

Everyone had the same space frame chassis and it had been specifically designed for the series in 1986. Saab 2.2 turbo engines were used. You're talking about a proper single-seater racing car and the series was extremely competitive.

The philosophy behind it is to develop drivers and have them compete on as equal a footing as possible while at the same time allowing them some tuning adjustments but not really engineering adjustments. The gearbox ratios are fixed, the power is fixed, the weight is ballasted, the ride heights are dictated, the spring rates are dictated and so on. Effectively what you have is driver adjustments – wing angles and so on – and some movement on tyre pressures but, at the end of the day, you end up with a bunch of kids running cars which are prepared as identically as possible.

It's trying to eliminate variables at that point in a career and often means you have 12 to 15 cars on the grid who've done times within the same second. In a race you'd have, say, 24 cars. That's a good number, depending on the event. At that time we could run as high as 26 or as low as 19 or 20.

Once the guys leave this series they are instantly competitive at the next level, in Formula Atlantic or even Indy Lights. It was comparable in philosophy to Palmer Audi:[5] the relative speed of the cars and where the formula sits within Europe is analogous.

I first met Montoya in 1994, probably in winter testing, which usually started in February or March. The first race, and my first real memory of all that, was the Miami Grand Prix on the old downtown street circuit using Biscayne Boulevard [near the shoreline]. If I'm not mistaken he was on pole…

Waddell is mistaken but only slightly. Pole went to Jerry Nadeau[6] with Montoya on what Elford delightfully describes as 'the outside pole' – the front row. He might even have had pole itself but, as Elford points out, 'some drivers had raced there before and Montoya, of course, had not. It was a full schedule for the weekend and it rained occasionally so practice was limited. Nadeau was already an experienced competitor.'

'At that time,' Waddell says, 'his English was very weak, almost non-existent. There wasn't a lot of communication. He was there on the front row so

Welcome to Britain! Sir Jackie Stewart and Montoya prepare for the Formula Vauxhall season, 1995. (LAT)

quickly and I don't recall wondering where he'd come from or what his history was but I do remember thinking he had definitely made a statement at the very beginning. You could tell – just like today – by the way he carried his body, that he was supremely confident and not to be intimidated in any way. He never even appeared to be nervous. So what you had was this interesting enigma: a kid who carried himself like that and all of a sudden he's on the front row. You don't know what you're going to do about it or how you're going to react to it. You think *well, OK, so he's fast. Let's see how he races.*'

Elford recounts the tale. 'When they came around for the green flag Montoya didn't wait [until the pole man had passed the flag, thus starting the race], he just took off! He jumped to about a five-car length lead and then, just like Senna, stayed there.

'Apart from a couple of Pace Car periods the gap never varied for the whole race and no-one ever got closer. He simply sat there while everyone else was tripping over themselves trying to get at him.'

Montoya led all 17 laps. It wasn't that simple, however.

Waddell explains that 'what Montoya had never experienced was a Pace Car situation and, without the language, it was all a little bit difficult. It was notable that at this time Skip Barber had just started to provide some level of coaching within the Saab series, although this was very new and somewhat informal. You had guys on the course helping out. Now it has grown to much higher levels and the coaches are doing data debriefs and things. In those days nobody was asking questions and what became very apparent on the first full course yellow was that he didn't know how to bring the cars back to green.[7]

'I can distinctly remember seeing the Pace Car lights go out and I was about eighth on the racetrack. When the Pace Car lights go out the leader's supposed to maintain his speed so the Pace Car will accelerate away into the pit lane: then the leader brings the rest to the starting line and off we go.

'Well, Montoya's not really sure what to do but he's

26

smart enough to think *because I'm not really sure what to do here I'm going to kinda slow down, wait and see*. I recall being at five miles an hour – and we had to follow him because we're still under the full course yellow. So we're sitting there looking at each other with our feet on the clutch saying *this guy doesn't know what to do*. We creep along and creep along and eventually we come to the last corner and there's the starter. He throws the green flag and Montoya knows what to do then: off we go.

'We get through it, he wins the race and he gets heavily chastised by the powers that be. "That's an improper re-start" and all this kind of thing. Well, of course, they assumed he knew what to do.'

That's not the Senna-esque part – *that* refers to the start, and what might seem an irrelevance: the race was being televised.

'Afterwards,' Elford says, 'I talked to Montoya in the paddock and I asked him how come he had made such a balls-up of the start. I'm not that big, but here was this rather frail looking kid gazing up at me saying "Oh, I didn't screw up, I did it on purpose!" I was dumbfounded. I asked him why and he replied "well, I knew that with this busy weekend and a tight TV schedule there was no way in the world they would [abort the start and] send us around a second time, so I thought I'd make everyone nervous." Did he ever…'

Subsequently, Waddell says, the Pace Car incident became 'a very funny story'. That happened at Belle Isle, Detroit, the fifth race, where Montoya led laps one to seven, then 'we're full course yellow again. Partly, I think, because of his by-no-means-submissive attitude, the officials felt like *oh boy, here we go. He screwed us up in Miami – let's see if he can do it right this time*. The lights went out on the Pace Car and Montoya started to slow the field just a bit, because now he's got a little experience and the track was awkward for the leader: a different kind of layout than Miami, and the guys lying second and third could anticipate the re-start [and get the jump on him]. In fact, it was the sort of situation where as leader you really didn't want to stay with the Pace Car, you wanted to get farther away from it than you should to utilise the last corner to your advantage: let the Pace Car go, let him pull off and then use the speed of the last corner to go at full throttle. Waddell remembers:

Montoya was smart enough that he knew what he wanted to do and he tried it very subtly by backing away from the Pace Car just a little bit. The officials were so sensitive to his potential misconduct that they started yelling at the Pace Car "don't let him slow down!" What the hell is the Pace Car going to do? Slow down too. So who's slowing who down now? Juan responds by slowing down more and the officials are now yelling at the Pace Car driver "don't let him do that! You slow down more!" Again I'm sitting there halfway round the racetrack with my foot on the clutch going this is ridiculous. *I'm laughing at the Pace Car because even if Juan wanted to do the right thing now he can't. The Pace Car's going five miles an hour.*

I don't know how much it was the Juan Pablo Montoya effect on these officials but it really was comical. We're all sitting there saying to ourselves "hey, any time you officials want to figure this out! Get the Pace Car out of the way and let us see what he's going to do – because he's going to do whatever he wants to do anyway!"

The problem with doing five miles an hour is that we weren't running full 100% racing clutches. When you have a bunch of youngsters there's a lot of driver abuse, so if things are going to break – like the clutch – make it cheap. Now we're down to burnout speed, two, three miles an hour. If you have a proper race clutch, fine, but at the time it was right on the edge.

And Montoya had Jerry Nadeau, now a Winston Cup[8] driver, right behind him – two talented kids. So Montoya's there, Nadeau's sitting there, we are all sitting there and I'm thinking nothing good's going to come out of this. Juan dumps the clutch, there's a big puff of clutch smoke – and we're still 100 yards from the start line. Everybody's dodging everybody!

Actually he didn't completely blow the clutch out and finished fifth. It was just a sign of where his career was. People ask "well, why didn't he win the series?" but that's the kind of stuff that happened. Because of the language barrier, even if the coaches were explaining how to re-start properly, how much of that did he get? If they were explaining why you definitely don't want to do a clutch dump but need to roll it right up to when the boost is going and then just go, how much of that did he get? He'd make these kind of young kid mistakes – but the brilliance you could tell, because despite his not knowing what to do, he knew what he didn't want to do when he was stuck behind the Pace Car. In other words he had a racer's brain – he thought strategically.

The situation was that he was young, there was just enough of the language barrier that he became vulnerable to procedural changes [in the races] and it ended up costing him positions here and there as the year went along. It had nothing to do with his speed, his tenacity or anything like that, it was just an unfamiliar country, an unfamiliarity with North American racing – and new tracks every weekend. A lot of his competitors had both experience and track knowledge. His English got better over the year.

The coaches had absolute enthusiasm for trying to help him and many of them believed he was potentially exceptional even at that point. His abilities were evident but like all those young guys that really have strong ability, it's how far can he go with it?

He is not concerned in any way with making friends with fellow competitors or, if he was, it wasn't evident. I think he is the same today. From what I can tell, his friends are from his personal life, not at the racetrack. That's work, and I don't think he sees any benefit being close friends with any of his competitors.

There was another Colombian in the series, Diego Guzman, an older guy and very competitive. He'd been there for two years already and he ended up winning the championship strictly on being more mature and more experienced about North America, the car, the language. They had a very bitter rivalry going back home and I can distinctly remember both of them every session stopping in the pit lane, jumping out of the car and running to the Media Centre to call the local papers in Colombia. It seemed to be very important to them to get their story out first there.

The rumour was that there were two major newspapers in Bogotá, one a Montoya fan and the other a Guzman fan. Literally, the two papers would be more than happy to try to talk negatively about the other driver – so there was also a war between the newspapers. That's why Montoya and Guzman were ringing them, and whatever story came out first became accepted as the truth, whatever came after was just a cover up. That was their race within a race!

All we could make out of the whole thing was that these two guys were trying to curry favour with the rest of Colombia and it escalated into a very interesting story at Mid-Ohio [on August 13], where he won his second race that year. I forget who Guzman was sponsored by but his car ran in a basic theme of the Colombian colours: red, yellow and blue on the wings and sidepods. Montoya ran a white car with some sponsorship on the side, a liquor named Nectar which was made in Colombia. This was also the year of the soccer World Cup in the States and Colombia was highly favoured. They were beaten and when they got home one of the Colombian players was killed...'

Colombia had been drawn in Group A and finished bottom of it. They lost 2-1 to the United States, thanks to an own goal by Colombian defender Andres Escobar. The team flew home and Escobar was gunned down outside a nightclub in Medellin. All this could only have a devastating effect on Colombians everywhere and it seems that by the Saab round at Mid-Ohio in August Montoya was feeling the full effect.

Waddell says that 'we got there and the Montoyas made a very earnest plea to have the colour of their car changed: to have it painted quickly to reflect the flag of Colombia, but not in the same theme as Guzman who had the upper part red, then yellow in the middle and the sidepods blue. Montoya wanted to invert that.

'The story was – and we never confirmed this – that the Guzman people had started giving Montoya an anti-patriotic label in the local papers in the middle of

This is testing at Oulton: Kane and Paul Stewart are to Sir Jackie's left. (courtesy El Tiempo)

this whole World Cup thing: *hey, he's obviously not showing the country's colours, blah-blah-blah*. It got to those levels of brutal mudslinging. I can distinctly recall the mechanics scrambling to paint the car – *listen, it's very important that we have the colours*. We felt *what's the big deal*? As a competitor I knew the organisers pretty well and I said to them "he's Colombian and it's important. Whatever we've got to do we've got to do it."'

I asked Waddell, who has taught and competed against some leading drivers, to evaluate Montoya.

'Over the years I have tried very carefully to be a real student of the whole thing and not get caught up in any flavours of the month. When Montoya was there I was also racing Jerry Nadeau – a kid with no money but an ability to drive anything fast for one lap. Each had strengths and – somewhat – weaknesses, but as a

package I was never surprised that those individuals went on to have successful careers. I caught each one at a different time in a different place but they stood out in their own way. I hate to use the word but I must, and the word is *exceptional*.

'I never saw Jim Clark,[9] it's before my time, but the stories are there. Everybody in the States you talk to that was around then says "oh man, you just *knew* it. All you had to do was watch him drive one corner." As I was becoming an instructor, my peers were saying "we raced with Clark, we saw Clark." These guys like Montoya: you don't see *it* very often but when you do, you know.'

The *it* is a very elusive thing to quantify. On that subject, here is Peter Argetsinger, who worked with Waddell and had worked with Juan in the Barber Saab.

What's Montoya got?

'That little extra something. He's got the Senna-type ability. Like Senna he has that determination and that focus. The first time we saw him race, at Mid-Ohio, he was sensational. I saw him as a Formula 1 driver even then.'

Of the Barber Saab, Montoya would say that four or five of the races had been on the supporting bill for the CART series and 'it was a great thing to be part of'.

On a more modest level, while Montoya was doing the series he also commuted to Mexico to drive there, and I'm indebted to Rod MacLeod for describing this virtually unknown chapter in Montoya's career. MacLeod worked as a mechanic for quite a few years in Formula 3, went to Formula 1 with Tyrrell in 1984 and then to McLaren. He wanted to be a driver and began karting in 1987, moving to the junior formulae where he competed against, among others, David Coulthard, but 'it was the usual racing story, no money.' By 1994 he had reached Mexico where Montoya was poised to drive in two championships, Prototypes and Formula N Mexico.

The Prototype was a Nissan-powered car with a carbon fibre chassis built in Mexico. It was fully enclosed. Formula N Mexico was the invention of Alfonso Toledano.[10] It was the old Renault car that we'd used at the start of the Formula 3 international championships and when they became obsolete Toledano decided he was going to invent a new Formula 3, which he did with a Nissan engine in it – actually a similar engine to the one the Prototype was using. Formula N was the support race for the Prototypes and had poor grids. There were never more than 13 or 14 cars whereas the Prototypes had around 20 cars at any one time.

I didn't know Montoya. He turned up with a crew cut and seemed very young – he was 17 but looked every bit of 15. He didn't say much. He was with his father [and another man]: a Colombian arriving in Mexico with a couple of guys hanging around him bigger than he is, and obviously a few people were putting two and two together and making body-guards: this guy's from the cartel, the Cali cartel![11]

Mexico was one of those deals where he wanted

experience, wanted to drive just about whatever he could get his hands on and he was offered the drives in Prototype and Formula N. I think that was pretty sensible of him and, conveniently, Mexico was quite close to Miami, where he was living: a two-hour flight.

I don't think he had to bring any money to the table, I think basically he got the drive for nothing. The team he drove for was called Osaka, run by a guy who had been around for years in Mexico. They put Juan Pablo in the car – I think they had had some contact with his father.

His first race was the opening round in the Prototype championship, in Guadalajara in mid-July. He qualified on pole and that surprised everybody, but in the race the car faded. He was doubled up with a guy called Gonzalo Davila, Montoya did the second stint and finished up sixth. At Guadalajara he didn't do Formula N and in fact he only did four races in N against five in Prototype.

What was he like in the Prototypes? Very fast, could knock off a lap much like he does in Formula 1 – go out there and do it. He'd be always in the top few in practice, the first three or four. You'd be following him and in a race you'd say OK this guy's not that special but in qualifying he'd do a lap half a second quicker than anybody else. For his age it was a bit mind blowing. A lot of people couldn't understand it – I couldn't understand it, and I'd been racing a lot longer than he had.

If there's one thing that I could really focus in on, apart from his obvious talent, it was his maturity inside the car. When you saw him out of the car, when he took his helmet off, you went wow because he looked so young: much thinner than now, and a real baby face plus the crew cut. He'd be off to play with his scooter.

He was very impressive over one lap, not so much in the Prototype but in the Formula N races. There he really showed that he had a huge amount of talent. I remember a Formula N race at Leon when he started last because, for some reason, he didn't qualify. I think by lap three he was leading. Even with a weak and thin field that was impressive to behold. I never would have expected him to get to where he has in Formula 1 because it's very difficult to tell at that age, but watching him you were thinking this kid's very, very good. He was racing against Toledano, who had a lot of experience, he was up against people who were no slouches and he was making them look pretty slow.

I spoke to him only a little. He was extremely reserved. I am fluent in Spanish and we'd have chats, mainly about how the car was. There was very little communication as far as personal matters went, it was all technical stuff – probably because he was so young.

I still think he is very introverted. Although he can be outspoken at times, the impression I always have is that he's shy. Even when he was in CART he was quite amazing.[12] He'd still come up and say hi. He was quite a contrast. You could be having a conversation with him and he'd be very humble, talking about this and that, and then somebody would want a photograph of themselves with him and he'd blow them off, wouldn't want to know, and that I found very strange.

Mexico is one of the few places in the world where, if you are a foreigner, they treat you with more respect and politeness and warmth than if you are from Mexico itself. It's a very curious place. I have felt, and Juan Pablo would have felt when he came, that you have contact with wealthy people in your daily life as a driver. That lifestyle and everything that goes with it is very appealing.

He was getting a lot of attention, he was winning races – which the Press love – and it would help him grow as a driver. The amount and variety of machinery he drove in that one year does your confidence an immense amount of good. The fact that at 17 he could get in just about anything and be a front runner against men showed his maturity.

That maturity was soon to be tested on a completely different stage – Europe. The Montoyas had on hand a valuable adviser in Peter Argetsinger. 'In 1994 I acted as a driver-coach and became good friends with his dad. Juan could speak English well enough that you could communicate although he certainly wouldn't get up and give a speech.' Argetsinger knew about European racing and more specifically British racing. It was to prove crucial.

Waddell regarded Montoya's move to Europe as perhaps inevitable. 'It surprised no-one and we knew, as long as he had proper equipment, he was going to be competitive right out of the box. Peter Argetsinger escorted the family over and introduced them to Paul Stewart. He was familiar with Jackie Stewart from years gone by.[13] It was not a warm reception right away but Pete said "trust me, this kid's the real deal. It's worth your time to pay attention here."'

He was not wrong.

NOTES

1. The Skip Barber Racing School gives lessons at 20 of America's leading circuits. The Sears Point International Raceway is a 2.52-mile (4.05km) circuit in California.
2. It was Ronnie Bucknum who drove the Honda when it entered Grand Prix racing in 1964.
3. Outstanding Brazilian prospect.
4. Formula Ford 2000, the junior formula in which Ayrton Senna competed in 1982.
5. Formula Atlantic, an open-wheel series useful to young drivers; Indy Lights, a junior racing car series; Palmer Audi, a British series designed to encourage young drivers by making it affordable and giving them the same equiment.
6. Nadeau, a versatile American with extensive European experience.
7. The leader controlling the cars from the Pace Car pulling off to the green flag.
8. Winston Cup, a NASCAR (National Association for Stock Car Auto Racing) series.
9. Jim Clark won the Indy 500 in 1963, and the Milwaukee 500, apart from his doings in the United States Grands Prix.
10. Alfonso Toledano, a Mexican who was a contemporary of Senna in the early days in Britain.
11. Cali is the Colombian centre for drugs.
12. CART is also known as Champ Car Racing but for simplicity I have called it CART throughout. It broke away from IndyCar racing in the mid-1990s.
13. Everybody knows the Stewart family: Sir Jackie, Helen, sons Paul and Mark.

It's 1995.
Montoya is
preparing to take
three poles and
three race wins in
Formula Vauxhall.
He would finish
third in the
championship.
(LAT)

boys will
be boys

'I knew the best racing ladder in the world was in England and I wanted to beat the best so I came here in 1995.' Montoya's words carry a simple logic but embrace a subtle choice. He could have remained in the United States and got onto *that* ladder – perhaps Indy Lights – but it would have made Formula 1 more elusive.

Fortunately, Argetsinger was on hand to give advice. 'I'd worked in England for 11 years and was chief instructor at Brands Hatch. I'd raced Formula Ford, I'd raced Formula 3 in 1982, I'd worked with guys like Damon Hill. Juan was clearly a special talent. I knew Jackie Stewart and I thought that would be the team.'

Stewart, thrice World Champion, had helped son Paul set up Paul Stewart Racing in 1988. This served two functions: to further Paul's driving career and to establish what Stewart described as a staircase of talent to bring on other young drivers. Argetsinger felt this would be ideal for Montoya.

Argetsinger remembers that 'basically dad asked me "should we try to do Indy Lights or go to Europe and try Formula 3?" I said "go to England, do Formula 3 and give it three years. If it doesn't work out you can always come back to the States and the experience will have been good for you." I said England because that's where I raced and I still think British Formula 3 is where everybody has to go if they want to get into Formula 1. In the Saabs he'd had an excellent season and was always a contender to win the races, but that was a stepping-stone and he needed to move on.

'There are lots of talented people who don't make it, but I absolutely thought Juan Pablo would go all the way, given the right opportunities. He definitely had the talent.'

The Montoyas decided on Formula 3, but the Stewart team already had its two drivers for 1995, the Brazilian Helio Castro Neves and the Briton Ralph Firman. Stewart, however, also competed in Formula Vauxhall – a rung below Formula 3 – and a seat was vacant there.

'Jackie really felt that Juan needed to do a season in a junior formula first,' Argetsinger says. 'Jackie was very enthusiastic. I knew Jackie from Watkins Glen when I was a kid[1], and from Brands Hatch. Paul was a little sceptical but Jackie listened to me and once they saw him drive his talent spoke for itself. There was a test at Silverstone and Juan was immediately impressive. I know that Jackie was very impressed, not only with his ability but the way he applied himself. He is a very dedicated guy and he's got a very determined approach.' Paul Stewart says:

At that time we used to test quite a lot of drivers, especially for Formula Vauxhall. It was almost more difficult than Formula 3, because it was a second team. If we felt we had good drivers in our Vauxhall team who were being beaten by other drivers we'd think we wanted that driver versus the driver that's in our own team. We were fairly mercenary about the drivers we wanted to pick – because we wanted to win. That was the mission of the company, if you like. I knew Juan had been racing in Barber Saab so we agreed to give him a test. I can't remember the exact

33

ins and out of what brought us to agreeing, but he actually paid for a test. Obviously we subsidised these things: the overall costs. It was perfectly normal for the Montoyas to make a contribution to a test. Most of our drivers brought contributions towards the running of the team and if they were chosen as drivers there were very few who got free drives.

The money they bring in does not compare to the amount it costs to run the team. Some teams would be asking for all the money, which we never did, because invariably the best drivers have the least amount!

I suppose one of my main recollections of Juan Pablo is the test at Silverstone, which was the first time we ran him. I didn't go to all the tests and I got a call from Graham Taylor [team manager]. "Paul, we've had a problem at Silverstone. Juan Pablo has had an accident. He's OK." He said it was a big accident and I'm putting my hand up in the air on behalf of the company on this one, because it was

very clear that the brake pedal hadn't been properly attached. Whenever you are told there's been a finger problem – something that's got to be done with human fingers – in a car it's a horrible feeling: a mechanic's error.

I went up to Silverstone immediately and before I saw anyone I had a look at the tape, because they had footage of it all. I saw the accident and he was basically a lucky boy to hit the barrier where he did. I guess he saw that it was a failure, that something had gone wrong. He turned into the corner, hit the kerb, the car went up into the air and kept on going straight. It hit the wall on the outside of Luffield Two – he'd been coming down the back straight of the short circuit.

You're not very happy when you see any of these things. I spoke to the Montoyas and apologised profusely over what had happened. "Look, I'm terribly sorry. First of all, is there anything I can do at the moment?" Juan Pablo was absolutely fine and

M-power, at
Silverstone,
1995. (LAT)

Jonny Kane and
fiancée Lesley-
Ann. Montoya
tried mind games
– and met Ulster
cunning. (LAT)

the father was calm as can be. I said "obviously you can have your money back." I was totally open about it. Their reaction to it was no, these things happen. We still want to drive for the team.

I thought well if ever there was a compliment that was it. He could see through what had happened, he knew we were a good team and, as a company, serious and professional. That's what struck me. I said to myself this boy isn't daft, he's very level-headed – and so was the father. That for me was an enduring moment. It would have been easy for them to throw their hands and arms around creating a scene. They could have done any number of things and it would have been understandable, but they didn't, and for that I have always had tremendous respect for Juan Pablo and his father.

That was the one important thing: he still wanted to drive for the company and he would have been happy to get back in the car and do another test that day to make sure he'd impressed us enough to

warrant a drive. Therefore you've got to have him. I was very comfortable taking it to the next stage if he was comfortable. And that's what we did.

Stewart already had one driver for Formula Vauxhall, a convivial Ulsterman called Jonny Kane. 'Montoya tested and I'd never heard of him until Graham Taylor said that they'd tested him,' Kane says. 'It was some time in October and at Silverstone. He went well and then had a fairly massive shunt. It wasn't his fault but the car was badly damaged. Graham was obviously impressed with what he had done before that. In fact, several other people tested although I can't really remember who they were.' One of them was a Finn, Sami Lahokoski – the only one to be mentioned by *Autosport* magazine who carried a report of the test as a paragraph.

This was not the only test that Montoya did. Contact had been made with a Formula 3 team called Fortec, run by Richard Dutton – and Dutton had 'heard a lot about him because I was running an Indy Lights car in

1994. Juan was doing Barber Saab, although I hadn't seen him. He approached us and flew over. We did the test at Donington – he'd done the Vauxhall test with Stewart before that. Juan was in a Formula 3 car for the first time and it was wet. He impressed us by his car control which was just exceptional and he was getting the car at some fantastic angles.'

Naturally Montoya remembers that Fortec test but 'I decided I wanted to do a year of Formula Vauxhall to learn the circuits, because you only get one chance at Formula 3.'

Clearly this young man is in a hurry and, because Formula 3 can be a direct route into Formula 1, he does not want to spend a second year there: so, dominate immediately, move on. This strategy perhaps did not apply to Formula Vauxhall where beginners had the basics to master and if that took a second year, no matter. Once the basics were in place they would have to be refined but not essentially altered until Formula 1.

Kane's deal with Stewart for Formula Vauxhall was 'done early on and Juan Pablo came along in January. We started testing in February.'

Among the drivers Kane and Montoya would be competing against was a young Scotsman, Peter Dumbreck,[2] who says that 'Montoya came from nowhere, as far as I was concerned. He just arrived in Formula Vauxhall with Stewarts, which was the top team, and he looked to be quite quick although he did seem to have a little bit of trouble adapting to the car. It's not an easy car to drive, it's a different driving style than other cars. In Formula 3, for example, you tend to brake very late and carry a lot of speed into and through the corner then get on the power as soon as you can. With the Vauxhall you braked early, came off the power and let the car turn in – you were still trying to carry the speed but without accelerating. It's unnatural for a racing driver. Quite a few drivers struggled with that initially – me, incidentally, as well. It took Juan a little while but by midway through the season he was starting to challenge for wins and towards the end of the year he was pretty strong. I suppose Jonny picked it up quicker than Juan did.'

Kane came from motor racing stock because the family business was cars and his father had raced MG Midgets. 'I'd had moto cross bikes and stuff like that. In the summer holidays when I was 14 I bought a kart – engine and everything – for £350 and did the second half of the season. As soon as I was old enough I went

With fellow competitor Darren Manning in Formula Vauxhall. (courtesy El Tiempo)

Motor racing is a very professional business, even at the Formula Vauxhall level. (LAT)

into Formula Ford, raced in Ireland for a couple of years, had a couple of Formula Vauxhall junior races in 1991 and won the first of them. It was the same sort of situation as Juan: nobody had heard of me before!'

Kane became a works Swift[3] driver and in 1993 got friendly with Stewart team manager Taylor. 'He'd noticed me and I used to go and stay with him sometimes,' Kane says. In 1994 Kane 'won 13 of 16 British [Formula Ford] rounds, but there was an engine problem.' Seven engines failed during the season. 'With all the engines problems my name got tarnished quite badly. People started saying I was a cheat – but driving in Formula Ford is absolutely nothing to do with the engines. I felt very aggrieved.

'Paul Stewart Racing was seen as whiter than white. I thought *if I want to clear my name that's probably the best place to go*. The Vauxhall winter series was coming up and there were three races at Pembrey. I was on pole for each of them and won each. That was it. The Stewarts had seen enough. I did a deal to drive for them for the year.' So Kane and Montoya were team-mates.

Motor racing drivers are notoriously casual in their dress but the image-conscious Stewart team would have none of that. Hugh Boss was a sponsor and, as Kane says, 'did all the team kit. We always had to wear a Boss shirt. We were obviously used to wearing jeans and a tee shirt, and to be made to turn up to the race circuit in a pair of trousers, a shirt, tie and jacket was a bit surreal. The whole paddock made fun of us. It did make Juan and me laugh a lot when they first told us we'd have to be dressed like that. I'm not sure Juan was very impressed. Incidentally, he's got a good sense of humour and he can take the mickey out of someone if he wants to' – so those making rude noises down in the paddock perhaps got it straight back.

Paul Stewart says that the team didn't always ask the two drivers to wear ties 'but we did ask them to look smart and appropriate to the various occasions. I can't remember it ever being an issue with Juan Pablo. They were very pleased to get some free clothes, quite frankly. I would send them off to Germany[4] and they'd be kitted out there.'

Montoya and Kane were of course rivals. They were brave, ambitious and aware that they would be compared. Each one had everything to play for. This does not lend itself to human harmony.

'To start with we really didn't get on that well,' says Kane. 'I think we were both trying to establish ourselves as the lead driver. We were in our first year in Vauxhall and also our first year with the team, although I had hung about with them a little bit and my best friend Owen McAuley had won the championship with them the year before. So I knew them. It was basically taken as fact that you needed two seasons in Vauxhall if you were going to win it. For Stewarts to take on two rookies surprised some people but, from halfway through the season, either Juan won the races or I did.

'I wouldn't say I was ever intimidated by him. I was a couple of years older, I'd been living in England for a year or two already and that probably made a big difference. We all try and play mind games on our opposition and Juan would try and chat up my girlfriend Lesley-Ann, who's now my wife, to see if it got me wound up. That never really worked because

he had a very attractive sister Liliana who I got my brother to talk to from time to time. That seemed to wind *him* up! He was very protective of Liliana and whenever he started anything with Lesley-Ann I'd get my brother in. He used to run around going "where my sister, where my sister?" I'd say "she disappeared an hour ago with my brother." Liliana is married now, a nice girl – the whole family is nice. I think he was trying to size me up and see whether I reacted to it.

'How did I take something like that? It depends on how confident you are in your relationship with your fiancée, I suppose. I'd been with Lesley-Ann four or five years at that stage. You all try and use what you can to wind up the opposition, and that was one of the tricks he used. It backfired on him a bit.'

Conversational interlude with Lesley-Ann:
He made passes at you to wind Jonny up?
'He did.'
Did he have the smouldering, sexy presence of the South American?
'He did have a little twinkle in his eye.'
Did you extinguish it?
Kane (interrupting before Lesley-Ann can reply): 'I had more than a twinkle, obviously!'
Did you see it for what it was?
Lesley-Ann: 'yes, I think it was a game.'

Peter Dumbreck points out that another driver had 'a very nice-looking girlfriend as well and there were all kinds of rumours passing around that Juan had been there and conquered that one.'

There are many mind games that drivers play to unsettle their rivals, but a conscious attempt to seduce their partner is unusual. Did it work? Well, he failed to win the championship…

Kane didn't need to retaliate too hard as he started winning races before Montoya did and was leading the championship. 'The fact that I was beating him was almost enough and I didn't really have to try anything else.

'There is always a level of friction between team-mates. We were both quite young and from very different backgrounds but both wanting the same thing. He couldn't really speak a lot of English and often enough when we went testing he'd have dinner with

us, then go to bed almost straight away and watch TV. I'm not sure if that was his way of trying to learn the language and maybe he felt a bit out of it because he couldn't understand everything that was going on.

'He used to watch *Bananas in Pyjamas*, a children's TV programme.[5] I think it was about the only thing he could understand. He'd arrive at the workshop and say *Bananas in Pyjamas!* We'd all fall about laughing but actually it was not an unintelligent thing to do in terms of learning English. Mind you, he picked up a bit of English slang too.[6] He only ever ate roast chicken, [mimicking Spanish accent] *roast chic-ken, roast chic-ken*. I think he was scared of getting something he didn't like, so he'd always ask for roast chicken and chips. He'd ask for tomato ketchup and mayonnaise, and he'd mix them together to make Thousand Island dressing.

'His English came on massively during that year. I used to find it funny when a Colombian would come out with a Northern Irish expression. He wouldn't say "what do you think I should do?" he'd just say "what d'you reckon?" People would look at this guy who

couldn't string a whole sentence together in English and he was saying it with – well, almost – a Northern Irish accent, which was even funnier.

'We spent a bit of time together for him to pick up things like that. We'd share a [road] car to go to tests because he didn't know where he was going. He'd a left-hand drive Fiesta, ten or fifteen years old, from Graham Taylor. I don't think it had ever left Milton Keynes. Graham only used it to go about three miles from where he lived to the workshop and back again. I was in it with Montoya driving, yes, and he was pretty full-on most of the time. Thankfully a large number of the journeys were dual carriageways. I am a nervous passenger, but he was no madder than me! And it was only a Fiesta. How much damage can you do in that? Yes, OK, quite a lot.'

Kane's philosophy is that 'you do your proving on the track. It's people who don't race who try and prove things on the road, unfortunately.' In this matter we disagree, and I give him a list of Formula 1 drivers who regarded *all* cars as machines to be raced – in the case of Gilles Villeneuve, against each of the other four million drivers in Rio de Janeiro.

Kane discovered that Montoya doesn't make friends at the racetrack. 'I'm the same. I have friends outside racing and sometimes you want to get away from it. You're in motor racing to do a job, you want to beat absolutely everybody so why would you be friendly with them? Juan and I, as I say, didn't get on brilliantly to start with but that was only for a short period. I won the first round and then Martin O'Connell [a Brit] won the next five in a row so we were both getting a lot of grief at Paul Stewart Racing.'

At Donington Kane had led virtually the whole race while the 'impressively smooth' (*Autosport*) Montoya

On his way to third place at Snetterton. It was a lively race meeting that included some distraction at The Bomb Hole. (LAT)

finished fourth. At Brands Hatch two weeks later, in poor weather, Kane made a powerful start from row two but went off at Paddock bend and Montoya crashed at Druids on lap three. 'It was wet,' Kane says, 'and I went into the gravel on the very first corner. Then Juan went off. I just got back to the pits in time to hear Juan saying over the radio "I am in the bunker" – not the gravel trap, not the sand trap but the bunker!'

At Thruxton, Kane had oversteer and ruined his tyres fighting that while Montoya ran strongly into third place. O'Connell won easily.

Peter Dumbreck reflects that 'it was a very fierce year' in terms of competition. 'I had just come out of Formula Vauxhall Junior and I thought I was going to rule the world. I led the championship after three rounds and thought *OK, now I'm coming* and I lost it all: the car breaking down, getting into accidents, all kinds of different things. Montoya's always been a hard driver but able to get away with it because of what's behind him, in terms of backing.'

At Silverstone, Kane finished second to O'Connell while Montoya had a lively afternoon: he overtook Darren Manning and they crashed at Becketts when Manning tried to retake him. Montoya kept on, and as the cars behind closed on him he tried to fend them off

with some 'wild weaving' until he accepted the inevitable. He finished eighth.

At Oulton Park, it rained. Kane made another powerful start but went off onto the grass and rejoined sixteenth, was hit from behind and ran last. Montoya chased O'Connell and finished some three and a half seconds behind him. At Brands Hatch it rained. O'Connell mastered that comfortably. He beat Kane by eight seconds, Montoya nowhere. O'Connell had won five in succession, a record.

Paul Stewart Racing, as Kane says, was 'used to winning championships and winning races, and maybe they underestimated how much experience counted for in Vauxhall. With Martin O'Connell winning those races we were under a lot of pressure to get our act together. We had a bit of a sit down, Graham Taylor, Juan and I after six races and Graham basically said we have to sort this out, we have to start working together if we are going to beat O'Connell. We'd been doing our own thing: although certainly not working *against* each other – that would be silly – we weren't constructively helping each other. Once we'd had that chat we really gelled and everything came together.'

That began at the next meeting, Donington, where there were races on two successive days. Kane remem-

In almost all circumstances he showed strength in Formula Vauxhall. (LAT)

Taking the air at pastoral Brands Hatch. (LAT)

bers that. 'One of the things about Paul Stewart was he always pushed Juan and I against each other to see how quick we could go. At Donington, Juan was on pole and won on the Saturday and I was second on the grid and finished second. On the Sunday I was on pole and Juan was second and I won the race and Juan finished second. Paul Stewart spoke to each of us at different times. "Right, Juan, why did you not win the race today?" and Juan said "Jonny won the race, he was quicker today." Later Paul took me to one side and said "why didn't you win yesterday?" I said "well, Juan was on pole and he got a good start – and we were first and second in both races."' Kane thought *how do you please that guy?* Lesley-Ann remembers Montoya saying, when he had pole, 'what does he want us to do, sit the cars on top of each other?'

Paul Stewart is well able to comment on this although he can't remember Donington specifically. 'I think I was always very understanding and I always tried to give them support. I was never disrespectful because I knew that ultimately what they wanted was to win races. I would quite often try and put things in perspective for them because maybe I saw things in a slightly different way. It's what a team manager does. Whatever the situation was at Donington, I wouldn't

have done it without being able to back it up with reason rather than just say it for the hell of it. If you do that and are challenged, you look weak if you can't say "well, this is why."

'You've got to keep the pressure on, and that is something I think we did very well. Quite often when a driver came to us he was afraid that the other driver was going to get better treatment, because he was British or Scottish or whatever. They very quickly understood that they always got fair treatment. As long as they gave everything, we gave as much back. That would have been the case there.'

A curious by-product of the season was that Kane became famous in Colombia because Montoya was so famous there. 'Juan would fly home and there would be maybe a thousand people to greet him at the airport. He'd be there to do a deodorant commercial for television. At one stage I was doing more interviews for TV in Colombia than I was in England! He was big news at home and so as his team-mate I was big news as well. After the races Juan would do his interview for Colombian radio or television and they'd talk to me as well. I'd have a guy asking me a question in Spanish, it would be translated into English, I'd answer in English and then they would translate it back into Spanish. The questions weren't all about him, they were about me too. I probably had quite a big following in Colombia that year! There was the football team and other than that there wasn't much else in terms of sport except him.'

At Knockhill, another two-race meeting, Kane romped the first but crashed in the second. Montoya was fourth and sixth. At Brands Hatch, Kane won – Montoya third.

Of Snetterton, Kane remembers a telling anecdote. They'd been testing there and 'somehow I figured out how to take the Bomb Hole[7] absolutely flat – on old tyres, new tyres, didn't matter. Juan couldn't do it and he spent the whole test day trying. He never wanted to be outdone. It's always the same with drivers. If someone can do it, you *know* it can be done and you *have* to be able to do it too. The Bomb Hole distracted him: his whole test day was unproductive because he was focused on that one thing. Even when he put new tyres on he still couldn't do it, I could do it on old tyres and that freaked him out a little bit.' At the Snetterton race meeting, in qualifying Juan hit the bridge. 'He got back to the pits and said "if I'd finished that lap I'd have been on pole" and I said "well, Juan, the idea is to finish the lap..."'

In the race Montoya had another lively afternoon. This is the *Autosport* account: 'Going down the Revett Straight, Montoya pulled out to overtake O'Connell and the duo went through the Esses side-by-side. However, exiting the right-hander, contact was made, Montoya hitting O'Connell and Kane.' Kane hit Peter Dumbreck and Manning was involved too. The race had to be re-started and Kane won it, Montoya third.

This matter of crashing happens, of course, at all levels but the fearless and very ambitious young driver, exploring the outer limits of his ability in tricky little cars, is particularly vulnerable. Yet crashing does not seem to have perturbed Montoya unduly.

'He always had a couldn't-care-less attitude, which I think has helped him,' Kane says. 'If he did shunt he just said "fix the car." He was paying for the drive, and if he damaged the car that's what he said.'

Here he was, a teenager, far from home in a team with the name Stewart and all that meant. He's shunting a very expensive and delicate piece of machinery...

'Didn't seem to bother him. I've heard him say that it's his job to push and if you push you make mistakes sometimes. I think he has calmed down a little bit since those days, he knows now when you can and when you can't get away with it. Then, he just saw it as part of the job, part of the deal, if he made a mistake every now and again and damaged something. I think it was part of his philosophy. We all make mistakes and some people accept it in different ways. At times, watching him, I thought The Big One[8] was going to happen but he's got through that now.'

At Oulton Park, Montoya took pole and was masterful all weekend, beating Kane by a couple of seconds. Everyone was happy: Montoya with a win, Kane with the championship which second place was enough to give him.

'He did have good car control,' Kane reflects. 'I remember following him at Oulton for 20 laps and he was on the grass at least once every single lap. I was sitting right behind him and I thought *right, that's him off this time for sure* and somehow he'd manage to get back on the track. I finished about a tenth of a second behind him and as we crossed the line I couldn't believe the number of times he *hadn't* flown off. What is that ability to go onto the grass and get back? I don't know, I really don't. I suppose he didn't go off to such an extent that he lost enough ground for me to be able to overtake him. He did have an exuberant style at that stage which he seemed to get away with.'

Dumbreck adds to that, and perceptively. 'At Oulton Park – the short circuit there – he just blew everyone away. He was miles quicker than Jonny, as well. He won by a long way and I think that was when he really understood how to drive that car. That was him set. I was pretty down, I was having a very bad year. I couldn't do anything right and by the end he couldn't do anything wrong.

'Regardless of what car you're driving, as long as the competition is there it's bringing you on as a person, as a driver, as a competitor. That's what happened to him, but he was in a fortunate position of being pushed all the way through, so he did one year of Vauxhall, one year of Formula 3, two years of Formula 3000 – and he

The majestic undulating sweep of Brands Hatch as the Formula Vauxhall shoal set off for Paddock Hill Bend. (LAT)

almost won it in the first year – then off to Indy Cars. He always had that next step planned.'

Montoya won the final round, at Silverstone, from Kane, and that took him to third place in the championship. Dumbreck has a revealing anecdote about that. 'I remember at Silverstone a party of journalists were over from Colombia and they already knew Juan was going to Formula 1 eventually. They'd sent these guys over from Colombia because they thought he was *it* and he's proved that he is *it*. They came to me and interviewed me for a radio station, asking what I thought about him. It was as if they could see six, seven years ahead when Juan would be sitting in a Formula 1 car. And we were in Formula Vauxhall!'

'I'm not sure, to be honest, how he took me winning those races,' Kane says. 'He doesn't show a great deal of emotion. He was a very quick driver and the only thing I can really see that's changed is that he doesn't shunt so much. He seems to have calmed down. He didn't know any of the circuits and he always wanted to be quick. I knew the tracks so most places we went to I was quick straight away. I suppose it doesn't really take very long to learn a track but he did have the habit of flying off either testing or qualifying or whatever. I suppose he was pushing too hard. It always amazed me how Juan could get away with it – maybe because he had good backing. I think if I'd have crashed as much as he did I'd probably have been out of a drive. People overlooked the fact that he crashed a lot because he was quick other times.

'He still owes me about two hundred quid from an end of season party from Silverstone! I decided to take the whole team out for dinner, and some of my sponsors, and a Colombian TV crew. They all came with us. It was the one and only time I ever saw Juan drink alcohol. The team gave us some bottles of champagne: he and I ended up drinking pints of vintage champagne! He's a non-drinker but at one stage he couldn't get it into himself fast enough – it was dripping out of both sides of his mouth onto his Hugo Boss shirt. The two hundred quid was his share and he never paid up although *his* mechanics were there! I paid for the whole lot – but it was a brilliant night.'

NOTES

1. Watkins Glen, in upstate New York, was the home of the US Grand Prix between 1961 and 1980.
2. Dumbreck is a most level-headed man, as he proved when the Mercedes he was driving in the 1999 Le Mans 24-hour race suddenly took off vertically – giving some of the most astonishing motor racing pictures ever. He was dispassionate in discussing it afterwards.
3. Californian company which began making racing cars in 1983.
4. Boss, German clothing company best known in motor racing for being a McLaren sponsor.
5. Carlton.
6. Slang is (of course) a polite way of saying that young foreign drivers are taught the Anglo Saxon words they will be encountering soon enough.
7. Bomb Hole, a spectacular right-hander (Turn 4) at the Snetterton circuit, where many (including Mika Häkkinen) have come to grief.
8. The Big One is a shorthand, usually applied to young drivers, meaning a major crash.

In 1996 Montoya would finish fifth in the British Formula 3 championship. This is Silverstone. (LAT)

nickname, trigger

If you do need two seasons to win Formula Vauxhall, the judgement at the end of the first season – to stay or to step up to Formula 3 – can be delicate. It's not just a question of ambition but opportunity and momentum: which choice will better serve the career? A Vauxhall championship may be better currency than a mediocre F3 season.

Montoya did not dilute his original creed – 'I wanted to beat the best' – and he moved up. That involved positional movement amongst the fraternity of young drivers.

Logically, Montoya ought to have gone to Formula 3 with the Paul Stewart team but there was an understandable problem. As Kane says: 'My contract had a clause – I don't know if Juan's was the same, but I assume it was – that if I won the Vauxhall championship I would be driving in Formula 3 for Stewart the following year. I got the job done. There were only two seats available, they kept Ralph Firman[1] on for a second year and I was assured of the other seat.'

In fact, after the 1995 Vauxhall season ended, Montoya drove for Paul Stewart in the International Formula 3 Cup at Donington. That was October and in mid-week testing he damaged Firman's car, which he was borrowing. In qualifying he crossed the line on what the team told him was pole, only to tell him an instant later that he'd been relegated to second. During the race it seems his engine wasn't pulling properly and, defending his position, he went off and rejoined eighth. It was a typical Montoya début: speed, promise, drama. *Autosport* described him as 'the newcomer who made the biggest impact' over the weekend.

Stewart contemplated running a third Formula 3 car in 1996 but Montoya would reflect that, in the January, 'when we had the money, we were told that they wouldn't run a third car – but I knew Fortec had the Mitsubishi engine so I came there and I think I made the right choice.'

Gazing back, Paul Stewart says: 'Juan Pablo had been up against it in the Formula Vauxhall year, competing against British drivers [who felt at home and knew the circuits] for the championship and there were some good guys in there. There would have been a clause of some sort that if they won the championship we would give them a drive in Formula 3. We already had Firman so only one seat remained and Kane got it.

'Run three cars? We always looked at different scenarios but we were very worried about going down the third car route. It complicates things in the way the psychology of the team works. I rarely ever saw the overall motivation being kept up with three cars. You might have one driver pushing another and if you have a third driver in the equation he can get left behind. He drops off, he thinks he isn't getting the same treatment. We could have done it – we had space in the workshop – but it would have made it more difficult for us to win the championship and the mission of the company was winning championships.

'It meant that we had to say goodbye to Montoya and I remember that very clearly. He was the one driver that I can say I regret losing: there was no other choice, but I knew I was letting go a driver who was going to be a threat to us.

'He was fiery in a car, sure, but I never saw him being fiery out of it. He had the perfect opportunity to be fiery that day at Silverstone when we tested him! He was always very reasonable, very level-headed, very calm – almost like his heartbeat or his blood pressure level is slightly below others. He takes things in his stride. "Well, you know…it'll work in my favour next time round…I'm relaxed about it." He's like that today too. He rarely gives the impression of ranting and raving over, say, a mechanical failure.

'I don't think one should underestimate his father's influence and contribution to the whole process. His father is a mild-mannered man but he also has a backbone. He will duck and dive under all the fences and is not afraid of doing that to get the job done. He clearly loves his son and loves his motorsport. It's a great relationship to watch because there's a lot of humility in Juan Pablo, and a lot of humility in the father to be there with his son and do all the things he has while all the limelight is on the son.'

Richard Dutton – running the Fortec team which gave Montoya a Formula 3 test the season before – can't remember 'why we didn't run him in 1995. I think he couldn't get the budget together and he went with Stewart to do Vauxhall.' Now, in 1996, Dutton assumed Montoya would stay at Stewart in

Formula 3 and anyway 'we signed Guy Smith – who won the *Autosport* Young Driver of the Year award – and we had agreed a deal with Cristiano di Matta for the other seat, but he was struggling to get his budget together. We were way down the road with di Matta at that stage. We started talking to Juan – his father mainly – and they were confident *they* could get the budget together. Marlboro South America got involved.'

A Formula 3 car had, Dutton says, '155mph top speed at somewhere like Thruxton. The cornering speeds aren't that dissimilar to Formula 1 because they are very well balanced, very well engineered. They are light and nimble: the cornering speeds are much quicker than Formula 3000. The acceleration is, of course, nowhere near that of a Formula 1 car. The Formula 3 car has to be very light and very nervous to be quick, and that's its nature. They have phenomenal brakes, phenomenal road holding and are not necessarily an easy thing to drive. That's why British Formula 3 produces so many Grand Prix drivers: I'd say 70% of the grid, maybe more. You see Formula 3 drivers go straight into Formula 1 cars and adapt very, very quickly.'

Montoya lived that season in Peterborough, in a rented house. 'He had a lot of friends in Cambridge so

Triumph at
Thruxton: fastest
lap and victory.
(LAT)

They'd gone their
separate ways
but stayed on
friendly terms:
Montoya and
Jonny Kane at
Thruxton. (LAT)

by living at Peterborough [near the factory] he could come to the workshop and go there. It was a flat – he didn't have an old landlady who cooked him the full English breakfast! He took up golf later that year. I don't know if he still plays now but he started then. You wouldn't have thought that somebody like that would have done.'

The season began at Silverstone in late March with two rounds and they proved as convoluted as only motor racing can. Qualifying for both races was on the same day: for race one in the morning and race two in the afternoon. Montoya showed his speed immediately to be third in the morning but in the afternoon committed an innocent and understandable offence. He tore away his rip-off visor the wrong way – so new to Formula 3, he didn't realise that it needed to be done away from the air restricter. The rip-off was sucked into the air restricter and 'eventually cracked it,' Dutton says. 'He was on pole at the time and went quicker but his time was disallowed. He was obviously upset, as you would be, and we fought with the officials – showed them where it happened, and it was a genuine mistake – but they wouldn't budge. They gave him a ten-second penalty.'

His English was good enough to explain, in an interview, what had happened and when he said 'so I have to start from the back of the grid' he accompanied it with a warm but wry smile.

In the first race he passed Firman and Jamie Davies to finish second behind Guy Smith. Montoya's car control was evident and he held the power nicely in balance so that his driving looked smooth. Kane says that 'we had totally different seasons. He started well and I finished well.'

With the ten-second penalty in the second race, Montoya cut into the field and at one point, overtaking, was almost on the grass. Dutton says Montoya 'certainly passed a lot of people because there were something like 30 or 32 cars in the race. The others had the ten-second start so they were spread out when he caught them – half way round the first lap! And he didn't take it easy after that: you're talking about overtaking 20 cars...'

Montoya finished twelfth.

Smith's victory at Silverstone, Dutton believes, shaped the season. Fortec wasn't 'anywhere near the level it is now [2002] and the Mitsubishi engines weren't always as good as the Mugens.[2] Well, to start off they most probably were but by the end of the year Mugen had come back. Mugen certainly worked hard that year: they had a bit of a shock when we went to Silverstone and won the first race. Mugen didn't expect the Mitsubishi to be so strong and they raised their game.'

Leaving aside the rip-off drama, Dutton judges that Montoya was 'very special even if a little bit too aggressive in qualifying. He mellowed as the year went on. His engineer Paul Heath used to call him Trigger because he thought he was a wild stallion. It summed him up quite well. He was always telling Paul off for calling him that, but he was a bit wild at first.

'He went from Trigger to mellowing, which was good for him. I liked him a lot but we used to have battles because I was trying to pull him back all the time: get a choke chain on him, like you have on a dog when the dog is pulling all the time, and you're saying *just come back a little bit*. He'd be pulling in a direction, I'd be pulling him back and we'd battle a bit. He was so aggressive and he'd never give in to anything. It was definitely his way. He was a very headstrong person.'

At Thruxton, Montoya showed all his aggression in qualifying, putting together an untidy lap which was still good enough for third but then, pushing too hard, spun before the end of the session.

The race started wet and he seized the lead. From the second row he angled between the two on the front row, the car slithering. He pushed hard again and, despite the conditions, was taking virtually every corner flat, as he explained afterwards. He led the opening lap by 1.28 seconds, and that's a long way. By the second lap a dry line had appeared and his ferocious driving took an immediate toll on the tyres.

Davies drew up and now Montoya's ferocity was transferred to keeping Davies behind. Montoya was, Davies would say, 'all over the road' trying to do that and Davies moved on him at the Complex[3] on the seventh lap. Montoya seemed to outbrake himself and ran wide in a right-hander so that Davies could take him on the inside. Montoya's car understeered because of the tyres and he was overtaken by two other drivers. He finished fourth.

At Donington, he and Kane battled for the lead but Kane had gearbox problems and Montoya beat Manning by 3.66 seconds. Montoya said that 'before this race I thought the championship looked difficult for me. It's different now.' Davies led with 53 points from Smith (48) and Montoya (47).

At Brands Hatch, there were two rounds. In the first Montoya couldn't get second gear at the start and was sixth by Paddock then argy-barged with Manning at Druids. 'He swiped across me,' Montoya said, 'hit my front wing and spun me round.' He finished twelfth. In the second he drove round the outside of Frenchman Nicolas Minassian at Druids on lap 2 after 'intimidating the Frenchman' (*Autosport*) to the point where he was too defensive. Montoya set off after Firman, the leader, but couldn't get to within striking distance of him until the final lap, when Firman was briefly held up. Montoya was second.

At Oulton Park, Kane stalled on the line – and Montoya did too, although one contemporary account suggests that Montoya had to stop to avoid the stationary Kane.

They were no longer team-mates, of course, and so 'obviously I didn't see so much of him, although we still talked to each other quite a bit,' Kane says. 'I'm not really sure if he did mature as the season went on. He'd win one race and then fly off the track the next. He was still a little bit on the edge and mixed bouts of brilliance with bouts of insanity.

'At Oulton I qualified on pole and Juan was fourth. We both stalled on the grid. There had been three or four start-line shunts [in previous rounds] so in the drivers' briefing the Clerk of the Course said that if anyone stalled the start would be called off. We were told that specifically. So we both sat there waving our arms – and they let everyone go! Luckily neither of us got hit, and we set off at the very back. For the whole race he and I traded fastest lap. He'd cross the line and set a new fastest lap, I'd cross the line a few seconds later and take it back off him. He ended up ninth, I ended up tenth. Everyone says overtaking is hard in Formula 3 but both of us passed numerous cars that day. We had a chat afterwards because we were both very annoyed. That was one of the times we talked quite a bit that year.'

At Donington, Montoya qualified second but made a hesitant start – he had a misfire. He ran twelfth, pitted and finished thirteenth.

'The cars have a power shift so when the drivers change gear they don't have to back off: they flick

Rural splendour at Thruxton – Montoya on top form. (LAT)

the power shift and it cuts the engine just long enough to change gear,' Dutton says. Montoya had crashed in qualifying but the power shift mechanism hadn't been properly rebuilt. 'It was cutting out on its own. There is a switch with which you can immobilise the power shift and then change gear manually but in the heat of the moment he forgot. He came into the pits and they switched it to manual, then he went out and got fastest lap. He was very often the quickest guy out there.'

At Silverstone, Montoya qualified sixth but the car wasn't set up properly and he finished seventh, although there was a curiosity about that: the car handled better as the tyres became worn.

At Thruxton, he qualified second and quickly shed the rest of the field. He said himself he'd made a good start and added that the race was then straightforward. Firman, nearest to him, finished 5.73 seconds behind. Montoya was now joint third in the championship with 91 points, Firman leading on 145.

They went to Zandvoort for a one off race, the Marlboro Masters, which attracted 85,000 spectators and entries from Britain, Germany, France and Italy. Montoya's car understeered in the slow corners and oversteered in the fast ones but he still finished fourth,

behind German driver Nick Heidfeld. That would have been fifth if Jarno Trulli hadn't gone off when something broke on his car. Belgian Kurt Mollekens won it from Kane, so three of the first four were from the British Formula 3 championship.

As Kane points out, the standard in the championship 'differs from one year to the next'. This is obvious but it means that assessing a driver's real potential must be done in the context of the standard in any particular year. 'Our Formula 3 season had eight different winners so one person wasn't winning every time out. I think the Marlboro Masters was a fair indication of that standard. A lot of people said German Formula 3 was taking over, but we went there and dominated.'

To which Richard Dutton adds that Montoya 'was definitely the class of that year and it was a good class, Firman, Kane and co. Darren Manning was nowhere and now he's test driver for BAR.'

At Snetterton, Montoya qualified third and ran fifth in the race but by lap four hard rain fell and, in just over a lap, he reached second: outbraking one driver into the Esses, out-accelerating another exiting the Russell chicane, then going side-by-side with a third through the Esses and taking him into the Bomb Hole.

A change of pace. Montoya at the wheel of a Mercedes in the Silverstone round of the ITC championship. He didn't finish. (LAT)

Eventually Montoya and several others spun off, and the race was stopped.

'In the rain he was fantastic,' Dutton says, 'but there was that little bit of something in him which wouldn't temper it a bit. He had to push 100% all the time. I think he got to the point where he was intimidating the others by his reputation. They knew he wasn't going to back off.

'I don't take many drivers to Formula 1 teams but I took him to Jordan in the August because that's how special I thought he was. I thought he was a future World Champion. I said to Eddie "you've got to sign this guy, he's really special." Eddie agreed to do a deal – "yes, yes, he'll come and test for us with an option as a race driver the following year." I was managing Ricardo Rosset, who drove for Arrows, so I was going to the Grands Prix. Every foreign race after the August meeting I'd say to Eddie "we need to get this sorted out" and he'd say "too busy at the moment, we'll do it next week." It went on and on and I lost interest in chasing Eddie. How did Montoya take going along to the Jordan factory? In his stride. Wasn't a big deal at all. Cruised in there. He was fine.'

At Pembrey, there were two races – he finished fourth and sixth – but Dutton remembers the qualifying better. Montoya was running a light fuel load, it was a short circuit and he only had so many laps to qualify in. Paul Heath was on the radio telling him to slow to create a gap between himself and the traffic ahead so he wouldn't be obstructed doing a fast lap.

'Paul could see the cars he was catching up. Paul would be saying "look, back off a bit, you're catching him too much. You need to find a gap." Montoya said shut the **** up, I'm trying to ******* qualify." And he kept it up all the way round! "How the **** can I qualify with you going on and on? Just shut the **** up." It was so funny.

'There were other times, however, when something was happening and Paul was getting excited but Montoya's voice came over very calm. He might be going side-by-side down the straight, might be banging wheels and this voice would be saying "it's no problem, Paul."

'Juan's greatest strength is the mind. You'd be testing and another team would come out with something new on their car. He'd ask "why haven't we got that?" Paul would say "we didn't know about it," or whatever. Juan would say "doesn't matter, Paul. We don't need that. I'm quicker than they are anyway." Some drivers would get upset that we hadn't got the latest. It never ever bothered him. He'd back himself to go quicker whatever they put on their car. It is not arrogance, it's strength in the mind.'

After Pembrey, Firman had 159 points, Montoya was second on 119.

They went back to Zandvoort, for a British round this time – or rather two rounds. In the first he took pole from Firman by 0.002 of a second, which someone calculated at one centimetre. In the race, wet, he finished fourth.

'He was out in front,' Dutton says, 'the others battling behind him. He had no idea what was going on in that battle. The others had worked out there was more grip round the top of all the corners than on the normal line: *because* they were battling, one of them would happen to be on the outside and they all saw there was a lot more grip. Juan didn't know this. He led right until towards the end and they all shot round the outside of him. He couldn't quite understand it, and the ironic thing is that in the wet he was so good.'

Firman took the championship at this race although Dutton insists that 'if we had had a better team and a better car Montoya could have it. He was definitely the best driver. If somebody is aggressive and brave and quick, it's much better than having somebody who isn't. It's much easier to bring a driver back from those things than push a driver who hasn't got them. We used to try and calm him down a little bit because he was aggressive but his car control was such that he could always get away with anything. He could overdrive but because his control was so good it was never a problem.

'However something could upset him in qualifying – a Japanese guy got in his way, for example – and he wouldn't back off, wouldn't let the guy go. He *had* to overtake him there and then and he didn't care if he took them out. There were little things like that in the early stages: just a lack of maturity. He had this killer instinct, he was very aggressive. The mechanics and engineers love all that, love a man who'll take it on – a driver like that is very exciting to work with and very exciting to watch.

'In a race he would never back off for anybody. There was an incident at Zandvoort [in the second race] where he and Minassian crashed because neither of them would give in. *Juan would never give in*, he was always like that. It's very much his personality: nobody is better than him, he knows that and so he's not going to back off.'

At Silverstone, he qualified eighth and finished fifth. That included two consummate overtaking moves at Luffield and one at Brooklands.

Dutton insists that where Montoya 'really, really shone' was Macau, the international Formula 3 race of two heats after the European season has ended and where, traditionally, the best drivers from the different championships compete. 'He hadn't seen the circuit before and he pushed *so* hard. He was great to watch, fabulous. Every TV shot seemed to be of him: he was *so* committed.' Heidfeld plundered the first heat after Montoya had made a fast start, and Montoya stalled at the start of the second.

It was time to make another decision: stay with Fortec for a second season of Formula 3 – 'he would certainly have dominated it if he had stayed' – or climb to the next rung, Formula 3000.

'He wanted to go on to Formula 3000, which is understandable, and it was the right move for him. I helped him in any way I could. We had conversations on "what do you think of this team in 3000, what do you think of that team?" I did help his management, which was his dad, really. I pointed him out to Frank Williams's son Jonathan. I had a number of conversations with Jonathan about how I rated Montoya as the next Formula 1 star – and with people such as Murray Walker. Murray would say "come on Richard, who's the next star?" and I'd say "Montoya." I had no doubt in my mind at all.'

First though he had to meet and beat Formula 3000. It's no surprise to learn that stormy weather lay ahead.

NOTES

1. Ralph Firman Junior, son of Ralph Firman who founded Van Diemen International – a successful racing car manufacturer – in 1973.
2. Mugen, a company affiliated to Honda.
3. Thruxton Complex, the tight twists onto the start-finish straight.

It's 1997, he's preparing to finish second in the Formula 3000 championship but it wouldn't all be smiles. (LAT)

stubborn like a monkey

Years later, someone put the point to Montoya that in 1997 when he got to Formula 3000 he was 'hot-headed' and either crashed or won the races. He replied: 'I must admit I used to be like that … I learnt that to finish first, first you have to finish. Points mean prizes.'

True to the whole tenor of his career, his first year in 3000 would be a sequence of beautiful moments and detonations. He would drive for Dr Helmut Marko, an experienced Austrian who'd been in Formula 1 in the early 1970s, had helped launch Gerhard Berger's career and was running his own team from the town of Graz. Montoya's learning, Marko remembers, was no easy matter.

'I'd looked into his records,' Marko says, 'and I gave him a ring, said I would be interested in running him in 3000. So the approach came from us. Basically, we made all our agreements by phone and after that was done he came to Graz just before his first initial test for us, at Magny-Cours. When he came, that was the first time I met him and everything was already agreed. It was a big risk to take but I am like that: maybe I wouldn't have liked him and that would have been a problem. I got the impression that he was really, really quick – which he is – but nobody at that time really believed it.'

One person certainly did, David Sears, and it's necessary to recap a little here. Since the Bogotá race in 1992, Sears had been – his word – 'charting' Montoya's career. Even at Bogotá 'I'd had conversations with people about him and how wonderful he was. He was then 16 and I don't think he spoke much English. He was introduced to me by Felipe Santos, *the* rock band promoter in Colombia who was also his first manager and found sponsors for his racing in Britain for the first couple of years.'

Sears knew that Montoya's father, an architect, had sold a house to finance his son's racing, 'and they had friends who were in the fruit business, exporting it to Miami, so they got free trips on the cargo planes' [to the American races]. Montoya, Sears concluded, had had it 'a little bit tough'.

Sears was then running a Formula Vauxhall team and 'wanted to try and get Montoya into it but unfortunately Jackie Stewart got a whiff of him and signed him up'. When Montoya was doing the Mercedes race at Silverstone 'we ended up having a chat and we were looking at Formula 3000.' Sears now had an F3000 team but 'we hadn't got the budget to help him so he went to Marko.'

Marko describes what happened next as 'always a fight. Montoya wouldn't listen about his food.' He only seemed to like burgers or pizza. 'I wouldn't have cared what he ate but it was obvious that his physical condition was not good. I tried to make him work more but either he thought that it wasn't really necessary or he didn't listen. We had some indications especially when there was a change in race conditions, like there was at Silverstone. He was leading easily and after the Pace Car came out the race was re-started and bang, he fell off. It was some sort of concentration problem. When you are not really fit your concentration goes downhill and, of course, we were very disappointed.'

Silverstone, in May 1997, was the first round of the championship. A young Brazilian, Ricardo Zonta, announced his quality by taking pole. Montoya qualified second. Montoya felt he might have had pole himself because the car could have done it but he didn't understand how far he could push it 'until it was

too late'. In the race Montoya was visibly quickest, Zonta behind him, but he felt the car wasn't right. A crash on lap 12 brought the Pace Car out and, when it was gone, Montoya went off coming out of Stowe and smacked the tyre wall.

Pau was a week later and, evidently, Marko was still brooding over the Silverstone crash and muttering that he was regularly beating Montoya 9–0 at squash. 'After just ten minutes he was sweating, he had a red head and could hardly run and breathe. And I was 54! It was a real shame for him.'

At Pau, Montoya was in devastating form. 'He did a really good job,' says Marko, 'you saw his real potential – he had been racing two or three seasons in England, therefore he knew Silverstone, but Pau he had never been to before. I remember exactly his third lap on the circuit: he was already taking the right-hander after the start-finish flat out. It was the complete opposite to the others who were shifting down before it – and he had to stay on the throttle a while to sort out the car [maintain its balance] and only *then* could he start braking.' The race? 'If you look at the TV picture it was horrible! All the time he was sideways, all over the kerbs but … he won.'

He needed only the first lap to construct a two-second lead, loved the first gear hairpin (just 'turned in and planted my foot') and was lapping back-markers by a third distance. At least one of these back-markers disbelieved that it was happening and inadvertently held him up, assuming Montoya had crashed and recovered and they were battling for position. He eased off towards the end but still beat the Dane Tom Kristensen by 35 seconds.

At Helsinki Montoya's *other* side was in play. He was ferociously fast by his sixth lap in qualifying and feeling at home because the circuit was bumpy, like some of the Barber Dodge circuits had been in the States. He took pole but made a bad start to the race, brushed a wall and crashed after five laps. He got the car back to the pits, they repaired it, he set fastest lap – and crashed again.

Sears remembers that weekend. 'We had a conversation when he was in tears because Marko had just chewed him up for hitting the pit wall and wrecking the car. He literally reduced him to tears. Montoya said to me "can you help me get out of this situation?"'

Marko himself returns to the question of fitness.

Do you think Montoya was indifferent to that because he was a natural driver and he'd never had to be fit before?

Preparing for the Nürburgring, where he finished fourth. (LAT)

M-power, at Mugello where he finished third. (LAT)

'That is partly right, but there is a big jump from Formula 3 to Formula 3000 on the demands on your body. The steering is strong and you have to be fit. For example I had a couple of Formula 3 drivers who did very well and were winning, but after five or ten laps in a Formula 3000 car they got out because they were so exhausted they couldn't drive any more.

'Montoya wouldn't go to the gym but slowly he admitted – well, of course he didn't *admit* but he came to understand – that he had to do something. I remember I took him once to my house, which is in the mountains about seven kilometres outside of the centre of Graz where he lived. I told him to come for lunch with me: "we have to discuss something. Bring your running shoes and we can walk." I had salad. He hated salad – it was to give him some vitamins. Then I said "I have another appointment, I must go in the other direction and you run home to your flat." There was no other possibility for him, except to walk. He was furious! This is the sort of relationship we had.

'At the first instant you said something he wouldn't listen. He was stubborn like a monkey, as we say here. It was a big problem. For example he fell off in Helsinki after being a second quicker than anybody else and there was a reason: the start went wrong and he was furious – again! At that moment he couldn't think. If he'd overtaken people step by step he'd have been in the points – because he was so quick, even with the repairs – but he was so furious about the start that his brain wasn't working any more!'

How do you approach a driver in those circumstances?

'I left immediately for the airport because I would have had a fight with him. I know how he reacts. I went away and talked with him after he came back to Graz. That was the only way.'

The round at the Nürburgring, which he started on the second row, was washed away in torrential rain and abandoned; at Enna he qualified sixth and finished

Spa, but he'd be
disqualified. (LAT)

eleventh after a muscular struggle including contact with Max Wilson, a Brazilian; at Hockenheim he qualified fifteenth and now locked into a muscular struggle with Jason Watt, a Dane, and Jamie Davies, a Briton. This was nervy stuff and although Montoya subsequently claimed to have been down the escape road once, a senior Marko team member murmured that he'd seen him down it twice…

'He's a very good driver, we gave him very good material and we tried to help him,' Marko says. 'He would have won the championship easily if he hadn't made so many mistakes. One thing was fitness, the other was something in his mentality. He fell off in Silverstone, he fell off in Hockenheim and at Enna he was fighting 80 per cent of the race but once he passed the guy he was fighting with, two or three corners later he fell off. When the fight was over – a fantastic fight – for him everything was over, he didn't have the concentration to keep the car on the road.

Here he chases
Jason Watt of
Denmark.
(Getty Images)

Zonta was miles ahead up the road *but* Montoya only needed to finish second in both those races and he'd have had the championship.

'He learnt, actually. I brought him together with a woman in Graz who specialised in … well, it's not like yoga, it's going into the person, seeing what their problems are and then get them to work on their minds. In his case that was to calm down and make himself ready to keep his concentration for the race distance. He went to the woman, I think, three or four times – which is a lot for him – and then he said it's too expensive. He was a little bit short of money and I think he thought he had learned enough. The fact that he had gone three or four times was a big step.'

At the A1-Ring, Marko says, 'he did a fantastic job. He couldn't breathe, he couldn't get out of the car after his qualifying lap where he was in pole position because he was so exhausted. He had done something special, and that is Montoya if everything is OK. The race was the same: Zonta was behind him all the time really pushing-pushing but Montoya didn't make a mistake.'

Zonta piled on late pressure in traffic until a misfire slowed him but Montoya felt he'd have held him off anyway. Zonta 27 points, Montoya 23.5, and three rounds remained: Spa, Mugello and Jerez.

By the A1-Ring, Sears says, Marko and Montoya had 'fallen out. We were in Austria, appropriately, Marko's doorstep. Pablo and Juan Pablo came along to see me –

The podium at Mugello, and no championship. That went to Ricardo Zonta. (LAT)

The gunslinger, quick on the draw from fourth on the grid at Jerez, final race of 1997. And he won it. (LAT)

The big door has opened. Montoya testing the Williams at Barcelona in December 1997 and looking quite relaxed. (LAT)

we had various mutual Colombian friends – and said "can you help us? We need some advice, we are in a bit of a muddle with Marko." Juan asked "can you help manage my son because I can't do it all myself?" I said "fine."'

The rock band promoter Santos had helped raise the finance for Formula Vauxhall and Formula 3 – Sears reckons it at half a million quid – but, as the Montoyas explained, Santos was primarily a music man who lacked European and Formula 1 contacts. Although Sears's team was racing against Marko's he said he would manage him. That wouldn't be immediately. What Sears said was '"Yes, I'm going to do it" because I believed the guy was fantastically good.'

At Spa, Montoya had a wild race which culminated in a black flag. He pressured Watt early on, and took to the grass at the chicane; then his front wing became loose but – running third – he sensed points and pressed on, holding up all manner of traffic behind. He was robust in keeping Zonta behind him after the wing disintegrated, pitted on lap 12 (of the 29) for a new one but stayed in the pit because he'd have been black-flagged if he had gone out. Zonta finished fifth. Zonta 29, Montoya still 23.5, of course.

Montoya was leaving Marko and joining the Super Nova team. Marko was preparing to stop 3000 and, anyway, 'I didn't want to go on with him. We were talking generally about it but we had two different opinions. Our characters were too different.'

Mugello proved decisive – Zonta won (and although there were protests about the legality of his car, these were not upheld). Montoya, third, felt sure he could have pushed Zonta but said he had a broken exhaust.

Richard Dutton doesn't think that 'Marko was the right environment for Juan because Marko is a very excitable sort of guy and there were occasions when he was on the radio shouting and screaming for Juan to push harder, and you just didn't do that, *never ever*. He was absolutely on the limits and there was *never ever* a time when you needed him to push harder. You *never ever* held out a board saying SPEED UP. This guy only knows one thing and if you push him any harder he's going to go in the wall, that's for sure.'

Marko is specific that only once did he feel Montoya was not pushing hard enough: Mugello. He does not know why. The last race was Jerez, which Montoya won at a canter.

In the background, emotions stirred. 'We had a hospitality unit,' Sears says, 'and because Juan Pablo had gone and told Marko that he didn't want to sign a management contract and was going to sign with me, his parents and little brother and everybody were apparently thrown out of Marko's hospitality. So Juan Pablo turned up at mine. It was the last race of that year and we won the championship with Ricardo Zonta.'

Montoya owed 'a hundred grand' to Marko, Sears says, and didn't have that kind of money. 'In the end I got the money sorted to pay off Marko,' Sears says. Sears would do better than that. He'd secure him a testing contract with Williams and 'I got some money out of Frank for him.'

Jerez had been October. A month later, over a couple of days at Barcelona, Williams fielded four drivers so that one could be picked as their official test driver for 1998: Montoya, Minassian, Soheil Aiello and Max Wilson. Montoya was fastest with a 1m 19.22s. This was interwoven into a standard Formula 1 test session – Jacques Villeneuve (Williams), Johnny Herbert (Sauber), Heinz-Harald Frentzen (Williams), Mika Salo (Arrows) were there, but handling 1998 cars. Montoya had the '97 and, overall, was a mere 0.23 behind the fastest of all, Alexander Wurz in the '97 Benetton.

A happier footnote, or rather two. 'I have seen him since quite often,' Marko says. 'We talk and have a laugh about the old times so I have a normal relationship with him. Why should I not be friends with him?'

'In Formula 3000 we sometimes fought on the track but I never had any problems with him off it,' Zonta says.[1]

For 1998, Montoya would be partnered by a Briton, Gareth Rees, six years his senior. 'We weren't friends because of differences in our characters more than anything else,' Rees says. 'He was a fun guy, he liked to muck around but …

'It was a professional relationship. Some team-mates I got on better with than others. With Montoya, our personalities kept us from ever being friends but we were civil with each other and we never had a problem apart from Monaco' – of which more later.

The relationship between team-mates is one of the most unusual and pressured in sport, not least because they didn't pick each other but have to work – almost to live – in close proximity.

'You'd leave a circuit when the mechanics were still working and you'd go off with your team-mate to have a meal together, so you were thrown together at the dinner table. A couple of times it was a bit awkward, again because of our different personalities. Once he'd done the serious business of driving the car, de-briefing and speaking to the mechanics, he would then unwind. He was given to fairly puerile behaviour which for me – being a bit older – used to grate.

'That said, if somebody gave me the choice "do you like him or not?" I'd have said "yes, I do." There was nothing to dislike about him – quite an affable guy away from the car. He was a blunt speaker. When foreign drivers learn English in Britain they pick up the Anglo Saxon words from the mechanics. He littered his conversation with expletives. I think he knew what they were.

'In the car there's no doubt that he had a little something extra. I'd had a successful career in single-seaters to that date. I'd raced with and beaten good drivers like Fisichella, Ralf Schumacher, Villeneuve and, to be honest with you, I'd never felt any problem with those. I always thought *yeah, I can beat this guy*. With

Juan Pablo it was different, particularly having access to telemetry. You share that and you see exactly where he is quick, where he's lifting, where he's not, where his various strengths and weaknesses lie.

'It became apparent that he was very quick and his great strength was fast corners. In medium speed corners there was no difference, really: sometimes I'd be quicker than him, sometimes he'd be quicker than me, but where there was a fast corner – I'm talking a fifth gear corner or whatever – he really was a bit special. He was able to carry something like three or four miles an hour more through the corner. This doesn't sound an awful lot on a lap time but when you look at it on the graph you see your speed going through overlaid against his and it's fairly demoralising. You think *I've done it as quick as I can – and he's quicker.*

'It's difficult to pin down what it was, isn't it? People often ask me that. Why is any sportsman good at what

he does? Why was Pete Sampras so bloody good at Wimbledon for so long? He obviously has something that clicks that you can't pin down. Montoya is the same, that extra ingredient of X which makes him special. It's also a good question if he knows what it is. I really couldn't say. I think he was probably driving the thing like all of us were – to the best of our abilities – but the fact remained, in fast corners his ability exceeded that of the rest of us.

'I was at a point in my career where I was a little fragile confidence-wise and the last thing I needed was to have him as a team-mate. It ended my career because it just blew me away. Maybe if we'd caught each other at different times it might have been different. But I've always maintained ever since that he was special.'

Montoya now had the Williams testing contract. Such a contract invariably means that the team rates the driver highly, and the endless laps covered in testing allow the driver to understand the discipline of repetition. For the headstrong, for the tempestuous, for the ambitious, what amount to lessons of control and self-control can be invaluable. That this runs concurrently with a season in Formula 3000 is not at all unusual.

Sears adopted a different man-management approach from Marko. 'Juan Pablo is one of those people you need to get your arm round. When he was having a bad day, pump him up again and then he'd perform. And as soon as he's performing again he's happy and funny and everything else. Another thing at that time, he was

having a really unhappy time with a girlfriend – before Connie. They'd argue just before qualifying or a race.'

There were 12 rounds to the F3000 championship and Montoya would find himself pitted against an ambitious young German called Nick Heidfeld, driving for the McLaren-Mercedes team, with all that implied.

Heidfeld describes the combat with Montoya as the hardest of his career. 'We were like rivals, because it was a very, very tight season. It was decided on the last weekend and that is why I enjoyed the season so much, even more than the season afterwards where I won the championship quite easily, if you can say easily. It was more fun fighting so hard against Montoya. I didn't know him before and although we had this really tough fight I didn't get to know him as a private person at all, only at the circuit and only by fighting against him. There was nothing like friendship in Formula 3000.'

Montoya was still a young buck. Consider Oschersleben in Germany. He took pole but at the start of the race was surprised by Heidfeld's speed: Montoya fifth and on the grass. He worked his way up to third but – the race had started wet – when he pitted for slick tyres the stop went wrong. Sears said that when they lowered the car Montoya assumed that meant *go!* but the right rear wheel wasn't on properly. Montoya did go, stopped, the mechanics made for the car and tried to secure the wheel but he went again. A couple of corners into the lap the wheel came clean off. Montoya made it back to the pits on three wheels and

You can drive
hard against
people and still
share a joke with
them afterwards.
Montoya in 1998
with Jason Watt,
who'd finish
fourth in the
championship.
(LAT)

He won
Barcelona, third
race of the
season, from
pole. (LAT)

later explained that this wasn't a problem *but* he'd been very 'frustrated' by having to go so slowly with all the other cars flooding past him. His 'natural instinct' was to chase them. When he had four wheels again he gave that natural instinct full rein and set fastest lap.

At Imola, where he'd never been before, he took pole again. He explained that in formulae like Vauxhall and Formula 3 you are required to master the unfamiliar – many, different types of corner – quickly, and anyhow he had evolved a strategy for that. 'I just attack them all as much as I can.' The race was pure Montoya. He didn't get off to a good start, spun and after 14 laps ran into Heidfeld. Montoya admitted he'd made the mistake.

He took pole at Barcelona, said what happened in the

previous two races hadn't affected his confidence, led every lap and won despite another incident with Heidfeld who claimed Montoya closed the door on him.

He took pole at Silverstone – four in a row equalled the record set by New Zealander Mike Thackwell in 1985 – and the race was no problem. Montoya 20, Heidfeld 15.

Monaco, a supporting event for the Grand Prix, offered a real chance for young drivers to impress the power brokers of Formula 1. That might suggest a measure of ambitious caution: battering expensive racing cars to bits against barriers might not look good. Montoya approached the Principality in a different mood altogether. He would launch a ferocious full-frontal attack and devil take the hindmost. The devil did, and the devil didn't...

Because this race weekend captures so much of the young buck it is recreated here in some detail.

Monaco was another circuit Montoya had not driven before, and it is notoriously tricky. Heidfeld knew the place because he'd won there in Formula 3 in 1996, taking pole and setting fastest lap. To balance that, no Formula 3000 had been run at Monaco in 1997, so most of the others were strangers to it too.

First qualifying, with Heidfeld for comparison.

	Montoya	Heidfeld
Lap 1	9:36.12	9:35.39
Lap 2	2:10.333	2:01.589
Lap 3	1:40.455	1:39.231
Lap 4	1:45.754	1:35.619
Lap 5	1:34.827	1:35.128
Lap 6	4:26.894	5:08.694
Lap 7	1:47.810	1:44.630
Lap 8	1:43.229	1:39.227
Lap 9	1:32.337	1:33.149
Lap 10	1:35.940	**1:32.321**
Lap 11	1:33.333	1:41.913
Lap 12	1:46.295	1:36.337
Lap 13	1:33.388	1:33.820
Lap 14	1:49.257	1:36.178
Lap 15	1:31.678	1:44.405
Lap 16	**1:31.315**	1:33.843
Lap 17		1:32.687

Watt had provisional pole (1:30.925) from Montoya, although there were five other drivers in the 1:31s. It's interesting, however, that Heidfeld's quickest lap came mid way through the session while both Watt and Montoya did theirs as climactic laps. Montoya was not instantly quick everywhere but he was invariably quick by the end.

In second qualifying Montoya showed his other side: awkward and stubborn. His way of getting a clear lap was to slow down – creating space ahead – and hold up any cars behind (Simon Arron in *Autosport* used the word 'cruising'). Montoya's defence was that if all these other cars were so much quicker than him why didn't they get by? The Stewards didn't see it that way at all and removed his three fastest laps. It left him with a 1:31.998 he'd done in this second session, now worth seventh on the grid. Juan Pablo Montoya did not intend to let such a minor setback inhibit him.

As the 26 cars came round to the grid – all on slick tyres, although there was rain in the air – Montoya prepared the assault. Watt made an initial break and led at the end of the opening lap by 1.3 seconds from Heidfeld. Order after that: Gonzalo Rodriguez, Jamie Davies, Stéphane Sarrazin, Montoya. Now Montoya put Sarrazin under what the official Race Facts bulletin described as 'intense pressure' and, on lap 15, overtook him cleanly at the chicane. He 'immediately closed in on Davies'.

On lap 22, Davies ran wide at Massenet – evidently he found himself in neutral. Rodriguez was some seven seconds up the road and about to get the pressure. On the way to him Montoya set fastest lap (1:31.602). On lap 30 he made his move at the chicane 'going around the outside – and then across – the chicane, the two cars touching briefly'. Montoya missed the chicane altogether, although he'd say 'I thought it was my corner' (and Arron wrote that Rodriguez 'pointed out it might have been had Juan actually bothered to go round it').

On lap 32, the Stewards gave Montoya a 10-second stop/go penalty for missing the chicane and that put him from third to sixth. He did not intend to let another such minor setback inhibit him. He came back on and took Sarrazin ... at the chicane.

Order: Watt, Heidfeld, Rodriguez, Davies, Montoya.

Montoya's full-frontal assault on Monaco. He's behind Stéphane Sarrazin at the chicane down from the tunnel, then he's passed . . . (LAT)

. . . emerging
from his stop/go
penalty. . . (LAT)

. . . and then
hustling Gonzalo
Rodriguez. (LAT)

Watt crashed on lap 41, moving Montoya up to fourth and with two laps left he attacked Davies at Loews – and hit him. Montoya claimed that Davies braked early, although, it seems, Davies wasn't so sure about that. The official bulletin said they 'bumped' and Montoya 'rejoined without his front wing'. He was back to sixth and a slow puncture developed in one of the front wheels. As the end of the race approached he 'slid' into Rees and the tyre threw a tread so that he crossed the finishing line in sixth place but without his front wing and on three wheels.

'Often,' Rees says, 'people try and create the myth around a driver, a Gilles Villeneuve thing: continue at all costs [at the 1979 Dutch Grand Prix Villeneuve had attempted to get his Ferrari back to the pits on three wheels]. I don't think that was the issue at Monaco. It was a lack of intelligence on Montoya's part, really.

'I subsequently found out he had been involved in a series of incidents during the race. When I came up behind him on the last lap I could see his car was damaged and was handling abysmally. I was a lap down. I had had an incident earlier in the race where I lost my nose and I'd had to pit for a new one – that cost me the lap so I was actually coming from behind to unlap myself.

'As we went up the hill towards Casino Square I could see his car was unstable. I thought *there shouldn't be any problem here because there's no way he's going to be able to brake where he normally brakes*. Therefore, a) it should have been a straightforward outbraking manoeuvre to go past him. b) I'm unlapping myself so I'm not a threat to him. c) we're team-mates. Given those three points I didn't expect too much difficulty. As we crested the brow into Casino there's a left-hander. I braked where I normally would and – unbelievably – he also braked where he normally would in a healthy car. It was just not going to happen and – surprise, surprise – he lost control, got out of shape and hit me. I was to his outside: he had taken the inside line. He collected me, I drove over his wheels and flipped up on two wheels myself, came down on the barrier doing substantial damage to the car and also a little bit to myself as well. He continued, crabbed round the rest of the lap, and finished in sixth place.

'We got back to the paddock and I didn't go near him. Half of me wanted to go and give him a slap and the other half didn't want me to go over because I knew I would give him a slap. Fortunately my girlfriend was there that weekend and did a good job of restraining me. She advised it was best to stay away until I'd cooled off. But because we were team-mates we obviously shared the motorhome, awning and everything else. We were stood I suppose within 15 metres of each other. He knew I was there and he made no effort to come over and say anything to me at all. I knew if I went to him I'd probably lose control.'

Sears remembers each chapter of Montoya's Monaco adventure vividly: the overtaking of Rodriguez at the chicane, the penalty, the charge towards points and then 'into Casino Square he drove straight through Gareth Rees. I had to laugh even though it was costing me money on both cars and Gareth didn't want to speak to him again. Gareth thought I was being facetious by laughing but I said "well, what else can you do?" The guy dragged the car back and if we'd lost the championship by one point I'd have been seriously unhappy.'

Rees had a speaking engagement in the town 'so I left and next morning I caught a flight and he stayed on for the F1 race, as a guest of Williams I think. We didn't see each other until we arrived at the airport for the next race, which happened to be a week later at Pau. As I was going to the check-in he came over and pulled me to one side and apologised for what he had done at Monaco. I think he said he hadn't realised I was unlapping myself – and I am sure it was true – but that really doesn't excuse stock car tactics. They are unacceptable in touring cars, never mind single-seaters. It was a week later so I had cooled down marginally. He apologised and I had to work with the guy for the rest of the year. There was no point in telling him to *eff* off so I kind of accepted the apology.

'It later transpired that Frank Williams had watched the race, seen what had happened and after it had spoken to Juan Pablo. Frank said "have you apologised to Gareth?" and, when it turned out he hadn't, Frank suggested that next time he saw me he did. It meant the apology was sheepish because it wasn't really from Juan Pablo, he was

Pau was the next race after the Monaco madness, and now Montoya drove like a disciplined professional. (LAT)

Overtaking Jason Watt at Pau. (LAT)

doing something he had been told to do by Frank Williams. I think it's not really in Montoya's nature to come up and apologise. He did it, anyway.'

This insight will become all the more authentic when we reach CART racing and Montoya is forced to apologise to Michael Andretti.

Rees expands on Montoya finding difficulty in apologising, and recounts a situation involving 'a similar part of that character trait. I do remember the team having a little bit of trouble with him in the early part of that season in the way he treated the mechanics. He didn't treat them rudely, he got on well with them and they respected him, liked him. As I said before, he is an affable kind of guy and any driver that gets results they love: he's making their car win and also they get bonus money.

'However, it didn't even occur to him that after a race he should go round and thank the guys, spend a bit of time with them and show some respect for what they'd done over the weekend. I remember David Sears having to take him to one side and say "look, you've really got to show a little bit more appreciation." After that he was more understanding.'

At Pau, Montoya – pushing right at the limit – crashed in qualifying after taking pole. A wet race, he cut through traffic so incisively that people murmured

of Senna. Montoya won it and now led the championship from Heidfeld by two points; at the A1-Ring ten drivers (Montoya among them) went before the Stewards for failing to respect a yellow flag [danger, slow down, no overtaking] during qualifying. In a delicious piece of racing driver reasoning, Montoya claimed that *because* he'd been quicker on a subsequent lap he *must* have been easing off past the yellow.' He was second in the race after some spectacular overtaking moves. Montoya 37, Heidfeld 29.

At Hockenheim, Heidfeld took his first pole and at the start Montoya – tenth on the grid, which he couldn't understand – tried to pick up places and put two wheels on the grass. He settled, and inherited third place when two other drivers crashed. Montoya 41, Heidfeld 39.

At the Hungaroring, Montoya claimed that Heidfeld 'deliberately' held him up in qualifying. 'He saw me coming and blocked my path.' Montoya craned out of the cockpit – as far as he could in seat belts – to give Heidfeld a rude gesture.

Heidfeld claimed then that all he was doing was what all the others were doing, carving out room for a fast lap.[2] Heidfeld says now: 'The rude gesture? I remember that one very well! Still I say that I didn't hold him up, I just tried to get a clear run for my next flying lap. I saw

The championship
decider at the
Nürburgring, final
race of 1998.
The start,
Montoya on pole,
Nick Heidfeld lost
somewhere at
the back. (LAT)

The chequered
flag. (LAT)

Done it! (LAT)

him behind me but I did *not* hold him up – and what was more interesting was what happened afterwards. I was in the pit lane and he came over to me and started shouting. His manager David Sears stood behind him. They were screaming and telling me what I did wrong, how stupid I was and so on. My team boss David Brown came up and stood there alongside me but we didn't really say anything because they were screaming.' The most Heidfeld ventured was 'cool it.'

Was it disturbing to compete with somebody who had a temperament like that?

'No, I really liked it because there was a sort of tension and it was not a tension I was afraid of. It was more like a fight and I was fine with him.'

Heidfeld won the race. Montoya finished third, saying that running with full tanks at the beginning 'killed my tyres'. That seemed to raise a different question, however. Arron wrote that although Montoya denied in public the amount of Williams testing he was doing, it had begun to affect his preparations for 3000: 'there were factions within the Super Nova team which felt his current familiarity with superior braking distances is leading him to overwork his tyres a little.'

Moreover, as Sears says, 'at one stage Montoya and Mick Cook, who was his engineer, weren't talking at all. They are both very strong, bull-headed characters and I had to step in. I wanted to get Mick to look at Montoya's point of view and try it his way, and Montoya to try it Mick's way, and then decide which one was the best. It could even have been a combination of both. My forte in this business is to be like the conductor of an orchestra and when they go out of tune I bring them back, particularly mid-season.'

At Spa, Montoya took pole despite being on old tyres when the circuit was at its fastest. He was forcing so hard that he spun and was all over the kerbs. He led the race but the gearbox misbehaved and, in Les Combes, he found himself in neutral. That let Rodriguez through and Montoya followed him home, Heidfeld fourth As someone remarked, Super Nova were making Montoya *think*. Heidfeld 52, Montoya 51 and two races left, Enna and the Nürburgring.

Enna was 'strange' – Heidfeld's word. Montoya had provisional pole but lost it because of yellow flags again.

The Nürburgring podium, with Watt (left) and Rodriguez ceding pride of place to Montoya, only third in the race – but the champion. (LAT)

Heidfeld remembers the race very well. 'We both spun on the same corner. I was leading, he was second and then I saw him spinning in the mirrors. I was trying to keep calm but already I was hoping for the championship because if he'd been out and I'd won the race it would have been my championship. I thought *that could be it* – but then he didn't go off completely. I was leading easily and I thought *how could he spin there?* And ten laps, fifteen laps later I spun just at the same stupid corner. I think it was a bit bumpy, the kerb was a bit peculiar. I never thought you could spin there, then it just happened. So he was leading and I was second or third. I was catching him. I tried to overtake him and I blamed him for pulling over towards me under braking – and then I spun [for the second time]' Montoya won it, Heidfeld some five seconds behind. Montoya 61, Heidfeld 58.

The finale at the Nürburgring, so exquisitely poised, was flawed. A check revealed that Heidfeld's car was running on illegal fuel.

'It was really difficult,' Heidfeld says. 'The thing is that in Formula 3000 the chassis, the tyres and every-thing was regulated – and the fuel. Actually we used some fuel which was legal earlier in the season, and which we still used for testing, but it was not legal any more for the race. [The fuel formula had been changed at Spa and, here, Heidfeld's team had mixed some old with the new by mistake.] The FIA said it was not of any benefit but it was the wrong fuel. Therefore I was relegated to the rear of the grid.'

That, of course, was bad enough but it made Heidfeld thirty-third and only 32 cars were allowed into the race.

'We asked – David Brown asked – my team-mate Bas Leinders not to compete in the race so that I got the last position on the grid. Otherwise I couldn't have started the race at all. By then it was virtually over, although you never give up and I didn't give up despite how hopeless it was. No chance to win the championship! Anyway, I started thirty-two and after one lap I was twenty-second.'

By lap 31 of the 45 he was up to eighth and rain fell, giving him, as he believed, a chance because the others would be more cautious and he had nothing to lose.

He pushed hard and spun, recovered. 'I finished ninth, which was not bad but...'

Montoya was third, then he and Sears clasped hands in the pit lane. However flawed the finale, the championship had been won over a season. Sears was quoted as saying that once the team had calmed Montoya's 'Latin head' at the start of the season, all was well.

'I don't know if I saw him directly afterwards,' Heidfeld says. 'I think I did downstairs below the podium but I'm not quite sure. If so I would have congratulated him even though it had been a difficult season. It's a season I like to look back at although it would have been nicer to have won the championship, obviously. We really had a good fight. You learn, definitely, measuring yourself against him. At least for one season you need to learn to fight with a strong guy. It's not good to reach Formula 1 – although I don't think it happens very often – with winning everything, karting, Formula Ford, Formula 3, whatever. The season afterwards was a bit too easy.'[3]

Sears remembers 1998 as 'a pressure season because Juan Pablo had finished second in the championship the year before so he *had* to win it. We were up against Ron Dennis, McLaren and Mercedes with all the money in the world and Nick Heidfeld, who was a useful driver. They'd the facilities of their Formula 1 team. We hadn't, and to be able to beat them... well, let's put it this way: any lesser driver than Montoya and we wouldn't have done, and Ron Dennis would have said "*that's* why I did my own 3000 team." There aren't many people that can say they've beaten McLaren. We can.'

Jonny Kane watched Montoya's progress closely. 'His second year in 3000 was when he started to learn *how* to win the races,' Kane says.

In the background Williams were signing Ralf Schumacher and Alex Zanardi for 1999.

After the Nürburgring, Montoya would travel to Barcelona to resume his other career, with Williams, at a Formula 1 test session. Knowing eyes from across the Atlantic would watch him there, and change his life.

Montoya had 'always dreamed' of reaching Grand Prix racing because he believed it was 'the absolute pinnacle of motorsport'. He thought 'something

would come from my testing with Williams but when Frank told me he was going to sign Ralf and then he signed Alex I thought damn, I'm done! F1 was everything and suddenly it had disappeared.'

Patrick Head explains the thinking within the team. Jacques Villeneuve was leaving and 'we suddenly found ourselves with Alex Zanardi signed up, and no one else. Juan Pablo was obviously very talented as a test driver, but when Frank and I discussed it we thought that to have Alex fresh back from Indy racing – without recent experience of F1 and F1 tyres – and Juan Pablo as a rookie was going to be too big a step for 1999. With that in mind we agreed we had to have a current experienced Formula 1 driver. Ralf indicated to us that he was available, or his management did, so we did the deal.'

David Sears explains the other line of thinking. While Montoya was winning the Formula 3000 championship 'we were obviously discussing options and strategy with Frank Williams on a weekly basis. We looked at it and thought "well, do you put him straight in Formula 1? Is he ready for it?" He certainly needed to learn how to deal with the media. He hated any interviews, hated speaking to anyone from the press because they always mentioned things about his country and he was sensitive about it.

'We looked at what we were going to do for the next year. Chip Ganassi came into the frame because I'd raced with him in the same team, in the 1986 IMSA championship. We got in touch with Frank who got Chip to come over with Morris Nunn for a test at Barcelona...'

So: Sears went there, Ganassi went there, Nunn went there and, of course, Montoya went there too. He'd drive. They'd watch him drive. It was all as simple as that.

NOTES
1. *F1 Racing*.
2. The Hungaroring is like Monaco, with so many turns that baulking (inadvertent or not) is endemic when a driver is attempting a fast lap.
3. The following season, 1999, Nick Heidfeld won the 3000 championship with 59 points from Jason Watt (30).

Presented by Nazareth, Penn yl

It's 1999, he's in CART and he's turning the series upside down. This particular victory sign came after his second win in a row, Nazareth, from P.J. Jones. (Getty Images)

'hey, slow down'

'How I first met him is a funny little story,' Mo Nunn will say in his soft, bemusing mid-Atlantic accent: within the same sentence he can sound English and American. 'At the end of 1998 I was going to retire. I'd been working for Chip Ganassi for seven years and he was trying to convince me to stay for another year. Alex [Zanardi] was going to Formula 1' – from Ganassi. 'It got to the end of the season and Chip called me up.'

Ganassi: 'Morris, let's go to Barcelona and watch Alex test in the Formula 1.'

Nunn, thoroughly fed up with flying: 'No. Chip, you go. I don't want to travel across the planet.'

Ganassi kept 'mathering' Nunn every couple of days.

Ganassi: 'Come on. Frank Williams has got this new kid Montoya. Frank says he's good and we could have him for next year.'

Nunn, who'd never heard of Montoya: 'No, Chip, you go.'

Ganassi: 'Tell you what we'll do, we'll go Concorde.'

Nunn had always wanted to go on Concorde: 'What time does the plane leave?'

This was a major and extensive test, in early October, with virtually all the teams taking part.

'We went to London from New York and then we flew to Barcelona, so my first meeting with Montoya was there. A lot of teams were there apart from Williams – Ferrari, McLaren, Benetton, Jordan – and a lot of drivers, Michael Schumacher, Damon Hill, Coulthard and so on. I could see the car that Montoya and Alex was driving looked pretty low grip compared to some of the others and I was staggered by this guy's car control.'

Schumacher was fastest with a 1m 21.93s, Montoya eleventh (1m 24.37s) and Zanardi twelfth (1m 24.43s). But the relevance of such times is important only in the context of testing.

Nunn, a Briton, started in motorsport in the 1960s, ran the Ensign Formula 1 team in the 1970s and went to America in 1983. This October day he was looking at Montoya's poise and potential, not his outright speed.

After the test, Sears says, 'we sat down in a hotel with Chip, chewed the fat, doing the bones of the deal on a paper napkin. We got everything resolved with Frank. At the time we decided to go to America there were offers on the table from Stewart/Jaguar, Sauber and people like that, so Montoya could have gone to a middle ranking Formula 1 team. My philosophy was exactly the same as Frank's and we agreed on the same thing: Montoya is a winner, he's a fast racing driver. He is not perhaps as technical as some other drivers but he is naturally quicker, so if you give him a car that isn't quite ready to win, he'll get frustrated – and he wasn't mature enough to deal with the press.'

'After a couple of days,' Nunn says, 'we came back on Frank Williams's plane into the south of England, then we took a helicopter to Heathrow, jumped on to the Concorde back to New York, and then Chip's plane was waiting for us there. And then we flew down to Houston for the CART race...'

That was 4 October – Zanardi finished second to Dario Franchitti, incidentally, in the race.

'I remember the [Ganassi] crew saying to me "what's Montoya like?" and I said "this guy's good. He could

M-power as the 1999 season gets under way. (LAT)

win by Long Beach."' That would be the third race of 1999. 'He won the Long Beach Grand Prix…'

Journalist Robin Miller, who worked at the *Indianapolis Star* for 33 years, says 'I'd watched Montoya on the TV channel Speedvision when he was running Formula 3000 so I knew who he was. Then Morris Nunn came back from watching him test and said "the kid was pretty impressive". He had that indomitable spirit that you've got to have, and that cockiness. He didn't give a damn about anything except going fast. He was pretty refreshing in that respect.'

The announcement that Montoya would join Ganassi was made shortly after Barcelona. He professed delight to be working with a 'great engineer, Mo Nunn' and ventured that he might even win a race in his rookie season because he knew some of the circuits and 'in every other category I've won races in my first season'.

Montoya's first oval race in CART, at Motegi in Japan, 1999, and he seems delighted by the prospect. (Getty Images)

Victory at Long Beach, just as predicted. (LAT)

With Mo Nunn, fatherly figure and deeply experienced in every facet of motor racing. (LAT)

Ganassi said: 'I watched him test alongside Alex two weeks ago in Barcelona and was very impressed. He comes highly recommended from the people at Williams who have been working with him for the last year. He has a lot of confidence and possesses the tools and skills to be a successful driver for us.'

His contract with Ganassi was for three years, with Williams holding an option on bringing him back.

He was testing at Magny-Cours when the announcement was made and immediately prepared to test the Ganassi Reynard at the Homestead circuit in Florida, where there was both a road course and an oval. There, Ganassi, Nunn and Montoya professed themselves delighted after he covered almost 300 miles on the road course, although wind hampered him on the oval. Nunn signed a new contract with Ganassi. 'I stayed for an extra year when I saw Montoya's ability. He's a character oozing with self confidence. I was his engineer through 1999.'

One of Montoya's first oval tests was at St Louis Gateway. 'We went there and we were doing two days, one day for Jimmy Vasser and one day for Montoya,' Nunn says. 'The first day we're running and Jimmy was quicker by far than the others: he did a 25.5 lap and there were no other cars in the 25s, they were all in the 26s. The weather forecast for the following day was bad so towards the end of the day, round about 4.30, I called Jimmy in and said to him "I want to put Juan in the car and give him a few laps because it could rain tomorrow and he wouldn't get a chance." So we put him in the car and his fifth lap was 25.8. I called him.'

Nunn: 'Hey, slow down.'

Montoya: 'No, I'm taking it easy.'

Nunn: 'Don't give me any crap. You're going too quick too soon.'

Montoya: 'Nah, nah, it's OK.'

What concerned Nunn was that 'on an oval, as you are getting up to speed you change your line a little bit and there may be a bump there that you didn't know about and you get caught. He wouldn't have it. "Nah, nah, no problem." It worried me so I said to the guys "OK, fill it full of gas" – that'll slow him down. They filled it to the brim and then we sent him

out again. I thought *you're not going to throw the car around*. He was still in the 26s but not so quick right away.

'What is that? Natural ability, just raw talent. You can have 50 drivers who will be around a second off Schumacher, you'll get five that are within three tenths of him and maybe you'll get one guy within a tenth – it's the extra bit that this one guy will have. Can't be taught? They teach themselves by their mistakes as they go along.

'The other thing was that he'd probably done 10,000 miles testing in a Williams so when he came he was a rookie on the ovals but on road courses you couldn't call him that. Anybody who has done 10,000 miles in a Formula 1 car isn't a rookie any more.

'Anyway, when we went to test I said no guarantees on how he'll do on the ovals, we'll just see what the guy does.'

Montoya's first CART race was at Miami in March: he finished tenth, a lap down, but enjoyed himself. During qualifying at the next race, the Motegi oval in Japan, he announced himself dramatically, as described in the Introduction, when he put the squeeze on Michael Andretti, then misjudged the corner, causing both cars to crash.

'After the race we had to sort that out because it's dangerous,' says Mo Nunn. 'So we made Juan apologise. We said "you can really get hurt bad. You've got to respect these ovals. You make one mistake..." This was the beginning of the season and we hadn't run the [American] ovals yet.

'There was no way he wanted to apologise but he did. You could see he was biting his tongue while he was trying to say it.' Overall, Nunn feels that Montoya 'decided he was going to set the record straight and not be intimidated by anybody here, the experienced guys.'

Montoya has said[1] that the Motegi crash was the biggest he'd ever had, 'when Andretti put me in the wall. I locked all four wheels to avoid him but couldn't. I was bruised – but you would be, too, if you'd hit the wall at 235mph.'

Andretti says: 'I think that was a lesson for Juan. I think he learned that the United States racing is quite different than it is in Europe – Europe is a little bit more cut-throat. He thought I was doing something to upset him. I wasn't. I was on a full load of fuel and he didn't know it. He thought I blocked him so he ran me into the wall and we both ended up crashing. I think he just didn't realise what the consequences could be. I was hurt, my neck, the whole bit.

'I was so upset I could have killed him at that point. But then in the race we ended up wheel to wheel and he was very clean. From then on he was the best guy to race against. I think he really learned a lesson there at Motegi, he learned about respecting his competitors – and if you respect your competitors, you'll get respected back. From then on we could run through corners side by side and we could trust each other. So it was a good lesson for him and ever since that moment I gained a lot of respect for him.'

Montoya qualified fifteenth and finished thirteenth, four laps down.

And he went to Long Beach in California, a street circuit.

He was slightly concerned because so much of the testing had been on ovals but, with team-mate Jimmy Vasser helping and Mo Nunn supervising, the car was properly set up and he qualified fifth. This matter of setting up the car, normally so crucial to the driver – who can be fussy to the point of fanaticism – didn't actually bother Montoya much, as Nunn will explain.

In the race he travelled methodically towards the front, out-braking Franchitti for second place with a move which brooked no denial. That put him in a position to pressure the leader, Tony Kanaan, who made a mistake: he crashed. Montoya covered the second half of the race safely enough although, trying to build a cushion to 'protect myself in the last ten laps,' might have pushed too hard and risked damaging the tyres. He was more gentle with the car towards the end.

Montoya, almost euphoric, described this as the best win of his career. He paid tribute to how fast Kanaan had been and how difficult to overtake. No matter. The victory was the *soonest* by a rookie since Nigel Mansell won the first race of the 1993 season at Surfers Paradise. From here on, Montoya would be famous.

He was once asked about that, specifically being

Colombia's most famous sportsperson. This is what he said: 'I didn't really believe it at first. CART races were (and still are) broadcast live in my country and certainly motorsport is rivalling football in the nation's affection. I remember going home after one CART race and it was amazing – people were freaking out. Little kids would see me and start crying, and I thought "Jesus Christ, I'm having a huge effect."'

'I think,' Nunn says, 'what helped him most was that the grip level in Formula 1 was nothing like the grip level of our car when Montoya got into it. Formula 1 had gone to treaded tyres and, for example, Alex didn't like them at all. We had softer compounds, more grip from the tyres and more wing.'

The fame increased at Nazareth, a difficult oval of less than one mile, where Montoya took pole and won again after leading most of the race. No rookie since Mansell had been this accomplished and none had won successive races.

He recounted how, when he was testing at Homestead in the winter, he'd been almost taunted by people who said *yes, but wait until you get to Nazareth*. He liked the track immediately. 'The other ovals I've driven on, you have to have the car right to go fast, but here you can push it a bit more and get more out of it.' In the race he almost pushed too hard and thought *if I go on like this, I'll be into the wall*. The kid, as Mario Andretti observed in another time and another place, is thinking.

When someone pointed out that he'd joined Mansell, he said cryptically 'Mansell is Mansell. I'm Montoya.'

Miller remembers Nazareth, and describes the aston-ishing *absence* of driver input when the car was being set up. 'You ask Morris Nunn how Juan liked his car set up. All he would say to Morris on race morning was "get it close, get it close, get the car set up close and I'll take over." It didn't have to be perfect, just close. Or Morris might change the car entirely from qualifying to the race day – change it 100 per cent – and Montoya would go "I don't care, we'll see what happens."

'He was undaunted by speed or walls or challenges or the unknown. It didn't matter. He went to Nazareth and everybody said "my God, Nazareth is a tough oval,

The consummate victory at Nazareth, everything under control. (Getty Images)

Tying up any loose ends before Cleveland . . . (Getty Images)

. . . where he took pole and won. (LAT)

The beautiful intoxication of victory touches driver and crew. (Getty Images)

he'll have to learn some respect for that." He won Nazareth the first time he saw it, his first oval victory – and that's a place it takes guys four or five years to learn. Why is it difficult? It's fast and very unforgiving: one little slip up and you're in the wall.'

Nunn expands. 'I remember drivers coming to me and saying "Jeez, your car's awfully loose on an oval" so I'd get to Juan and say "you're telling me that the rear of the car is absolutely solid. Why are all these drivers telling me the car's loose?" and he would say "bullshit!"

'As we worked through the weekend he wouldn't have very much interest in the technical side of the racecar. He'd get out and want to play the video games. I'd say "hey, come on, let's talk about the car" and he'd say "just get it close, I'll do the rest."

'He was no trouble at all to work with. No driver input? Yeah, but because I've been doing this for 40 years and raced cars for ten years in Europe, F1 and so on, I can go in directions when I can see whether the guy is going to go quicker or slower: down an avenue where you clearly see what the car needs.

'At first he used to say "I don't like the yellows, this is bullshit, all this stopping and starting." He's not the guy with the most patience and on ovals you have to be very patient.'

At Rio he won his third in a row and even Mansell hadn't done that. He settled the race immediately with a majestic sweep past Christian Fittipaldi into the first corner from third on the grid, and afterwards explained that Chip Ganassi had cautioned prudence at the start but when he – Montoya – saw Fittipaldi braking early 'I decided to go for it'. After that he pushed to the limit.

'Juan was very straightforward,' says Miller. 'A lot of the TV people and some of the Press people didn't like him because they said he gave one-word interviews – "yeah," "no," "I don't care". He'd shrug his shoulders and say "ah, whatever". But when you sat down and talked to the guy he was fun, very honest and always a

good interview. You needed a little time – when he has something else on his mind you've got to leave him alone. He won his third race in a row and an interviewer asked him "how are you feeling?" He replied "I feel miserable. HOW DO YOU THINK I FEEL?!?"

(The Ganassi team took out an advert in a British motoring magazine which asked: 'Is it still called beginner's luck when you win three in a row?')

At Madison he led from pole but the car's handling wasn't right, and got worse. On top of that, before his second pit stop he ran out of fuel, coasting into the pits and losing a lap. He finished eleventh. At Milwaukee he worked his way to the front but was given a one-lap penalty for overtaking under a waved yellow. At Portland he took pole and finished second. At Milwaukee the team had let him run hard and not worried about fuel: here they tried the reverse, to Montoya's frustration. 'I was going down the straight at *half* throttle and they said "save more fuel!"'

At Cleveland he took pole. Rod MacLeod was there. 'When I saw him in the CART series – I was working for Barber as a test driver – he remembered me and he still had a great communication with a lot of the guys that were still there. He would ride by on the bike and make

a point of coming in and saying hi to everybody. He'd just qualified on pole at Cleveland and that's what he did on the way back to his pits. It was refreshing.'

The race was wet–dry and he fought a long duel with Gil de Ferran. That was round nine of the 20 and the points had become: Montoya 112, de Ferran 87, Franchitti 85, Michael Andretti 78. 'I think winning the championship is now a realistic goal for us. I tried not to think of that too much before the start of the season, especially because I hadn't raced on ovals.'

At Elkhart Lake – 'a really fast and fun track' – he had gear selection problems; at Toronto he crashed; at Michigan, Kanaan held him off at the end. He had a brake problem, anyway, and had to be content with second. Montoya 129, Franchitti 116, Andretti 107.

At Detroit he took pole but there was something approaching internecine strife during the race. He led from the start and by 12 laps that had extended to seven seconds. However a yellow flag on lap 44 (of the 75) brought all the leaders in for pit stops – except Montoya. Reportedly, Montoya was not happy about this and over the radio demanded to know why. Chip Ganassi said the tactic was bold: *turn your fuel mixture to full rich and go for it. The others, stopping now, will*

He seems to be running strongly in Toronto, but he didn't finish after crashing with Michel Jourdain Jnr. (Getty Images)

The crowd seem to like him whatever he did. (Getty Images)

Victory at
Vancouver, four
races to go and
the championship
was wide open.
(Getty Images)

have to nurse their cars to the end. A sequence of yellows spoiled the tactic. Worse, he was hit up the rear by Helio Castro-Neves (Brazil) in a very peculiar incident, even by motor racing standards. The Pace Car was out but leaking fuel and headed for the pits so that another could replace it. Castro-Neves deduced that, as the Pace Car pulled off, the race must be on again and set off – into Montoya. It must be said that Montoya himself had no idea what was going on either. Franchitti won, and that was Franchitti 136, Montoya 131, Andretti 119.

He won Mid-Ohio at Lexington, another awkward track. This, arguably, was the best of his wins so far.

The car was changed for qualifying but 'we were still way off. I never expected to win.' He conserved fuel as

the race unfolded because overtaking was so difficult. 'I sat there in traffic, lifting at the end of the straights and getting the slipstream as best I could. I did an extra lap on fuel, turned it to full rich and went for it with nobody in the way. That was a good in-lap. Then the guys did a fantastic pit stop and got me up to third. After that, the car was brilliant. They said over the radio "you're catching them quickly" so I just pushed harder.'

He outbraked Paul Tracy (Canada) for the lead *on the outside* going into the esses. This moved Tracy to say afterwards: 'He doesn't worry about anything. He's young and there's nothing that bothers him. I guess that's the way I used to drive, but as you get older you think about other things: you're maybe not as fearless

Fontana and it was just what it said on the poster.
(Getty Images)

Fontana. Montoya would remain perfectly relaxed. (Getty Images)

November 1999 and the dignity of celebration. Montoya has won the CART Championship and is Rookie of the Year as well. (Getty Images)

that night working on a new set up and Montoya tried it for the first time on race morning. He led the race (225 laps) at quarter distance and for the final 40 laps Franchitti was never more than a second behind him. Montoya 172, Franchitti 168, Andretti 124.

At Vancouver he took pole and an important step towards the championship in front of a crowd which contained plenty of Colombians. He was surprised by how many there were: 'it makes you feel good'. He led every lap but one: it came down to a seven-lap lunge for the line and Franchitti, trying to outbrake him, spun into a tyre wall. Montoya 194, Franchitti 171, Andretti 124.

At Laguna Seca he qualified sixteenth and finished eighth after some biff and bash with Scott Pruett. 'I thought Pruett was an idiot, but at least I didn't damage the car when I hit him.' At Houston he took pole and was leading but Castro-Neves crashed and although Montoya tried to brake and turn away he clipped the car. Montoya 200, Franchitti 187, Tracy 155 and two rounds to run. The next was Surfers Paradise in Queensland and it went wrong there. Franchitti led, Montoya was trying to catch Fernandez and 'I braked and the rear tyres lost grip. When that happens there is nothing you can do.' Franchitti 209, Montoya 200, Tracy 161.

The climax was at the California Speedway, Fontana, on 31 October: round 20. It was cast into sun and shadow simultaneously, of the sort only motor racing can bring. On lap 10 the highly popular 24-year-old Canadian Greg Moore was fatally injured when he hit a wall. He died in hospital an hour later. The race had not been abandoned and, although the crowd were told, the drivers were not. Franchitti, who finished tenth, was so distraught when he learned about Moore that he walked away into his own privacy. It seemed utterly irrelevant that he and Montoya – fourth – both had 212 points, but Montoya won the championship on most wins. Montoya said it was a good feeling, of course, but 'today is really all about what happened to Greg'.

as when you're younger, and that's the way Juan is. They should put the Superman logo on Montoya's car.'

Vic Elford had 'kept in touch with his dad for a while. The last time I saw either of them was at Mid-Ohio. I spoke to them and they were just the same. I was in the pit lane and Juan Pablo was talking with Chip Ganassi and the other people. He saw me, came straight over and wrapped his arms around me. "Boy, it's great to see you again."'

Franchitti 152, Montoya 151, Andretti 124.

At Chicago (Chip Ganassi's new track, incidentally) he qualified tenth – testament to the fact that the team couldn't get the car working properly. They stayed late

NOTES
1. *F1 Racing.*

It's 2000 and despite an optimistic start Montoya faced a disappointing CART season – but he'll be in the hall of fame for winning the Indy 500. (Getty Images)

windmills of your mind

For the 2000 season Ganassi switched to Toyota engines and, in fact, mechanical problems thwarted Montoya's first four races: at Homestead an engine failed in the warm-up and another in the race when he was leading; at Long Beach an engine blew; at Rio the gearbox failed; at Motegi he led 175 of the 201 laps but a pop-off valve problem pitched him down to seventh.

These unexceptional races were in the nature of a prelude to something astonishing. Chip Ganassi had decided to enter the Indy 500, with Montoya and Vasser. That was extraordinary enough given the political background: CART had split from the Indy Racing League – and Indianapolis – some four years before. But what Montoya would do at the Speedway had them dancing in the streets of Bogotá and waving chequered flags hastily improvised from bed sheets.

Ron Green of the IRL explains the background. 'The very first year [of the split] – 1996 – the formulas were the same. In other words, when the IRL was created there was not the excuse used by the CART teams that they had to buy different equipment to compete in the 500. It was the same equipment. In 1997 the IRL introduced its own formula for chassis and engine, so if a CART team were going to compete from that year on, they did have to buy Indy Racing League cars. That was the only hurdle to a team, but they were reluctant to do that for just one race. And CART have had a race which clashed with the 500 at least once, plus they've had other races in May that made it challenging for the teams to practise and qualify. [This 2000 season, practice, qualifying and the race were from May 13 to 28.] There was, however, nothing to stop CART teams if they wanted to.

'Ganassi came here to the Indianapolis Motor Speedway with the experience of having fielded teams and raced here himself before,' says Green. 'He knew what kind of effort it took to compete at Indianapolis and he came prepared. He was not at any disadvantage to any of the existing IRL teams. We thought it was wonderful. Wonderful.'

Was it seen as a point of comparison?

'We did not. Many fans and some journalists did, but it's like comparing Michael Schumacher and Montoya, very hard unless people have equal equipment.'

On this, Montoya would say: 'I'm sure Jimmy and I aren't coming here (the Speedway) to show who's better, or if CART's better. I just came to have fun. Chip gave me a car. I'll just drive it as fast as I can. Simple.'

Motegi had been 14 May, a Sunday. On the Monday, Ganassi team manager Tom Anderson explained the team's plans for their first run at Indianapolis the next day, the Tuesday. 'Just to basically shake down the cars and get less than a dozen laps in each of the four chassis, then get the guys some rest. The bulk of the crew will be here tomorrow. They get in around 8.30am and we'll get after it in earnest tomorrow.'

That Tuesday, Montoya arrived and, in answer to a question about jet lag, said: 'I feel great. I had a great night's sleep and feel very rested.' The middle of the day was lost to rain but at 3.59 Montoya went fifth quickest (219.147mph) and at 4.50 quickest of all (222.104).

Journalist Robin Miller remembers that. 'I think the best story is when he ran the Indianapolis Speedway for the first time, and in an IRL car. He made his first 15, 16 laps of the Speedway and they were all wide open – the throttle wide open all the way round, never lifted. He'd never even been on the track before! He comes in, gets out of the car and sits on the pit wall. I go "what d'ya think?" and he says "my mom could drive one of these cars. No power. Downforce? It's a joke."

'Al Unser Junior kept saying "Montoya's crazy, they're going to carry him out of here in a bodybag. He doesn't have any respect for the Speedway blah blah blah." Somebody told Montoya that and he said "yeah, well we'll see." He really doesn't care.'

Montoya said the car felt really good, whatever constrictions the IRL chassis and engine brought. 'I am happy with the speed that we got in the half day we ran. We made some changes but didn't have a chance to get back out again.' He finished the day second quickest to Scott Sharp, Vasser third and a Texan, Greg Ray, fourth. Ray had been competing in motorsport since 1991 (he didn't have his first lesson in a racing car until he was 25) and this was his fourth 500. From here on, during May 2000, he and Montoya would be direct rivals.

'I didn't know him personally,' Ray says. 'We had had a few drivers' meetings and we'd bumped into each other walking through the pits. We'd had passing words, nothing very deep. When he came to the Indy 500 there was still some sort of rivalry between CART and the IRL. A lot of it was politically based and media based – but to a driver, if you've driven for a while we're all drivers, just as mechanics are mechanics, engineers are engineers. We all do our job and whether it was in one series or the other really didn't matter. You don't harbour any bad feelings.

'Montoya had won the 1999 CART championship so

Production line in Motegi but despite pole position he couldn't come higher than seventh. (Getty Images)

the media had made him head and heels above all the other drivers. I think he came across on TV and in the newspapers as pretty young, immature in some ways – cocky, kind of arrogant and fun loving. The thing was, he was always able to go out there and back it up in the racecar.

'He'd be in the pit lane sitting on his car – and he's like everybody else: as a driver you learn that your team is your family, and the more time you spend with them the more they work with you and for you. You build a chemistry. So he was sitting there and I thought it was funny because he would posture. When you'd come out into the pit lane he was posturing for all the cameras, his chin up in the air, nose high. He'd look down at you and smile – and it was entertaining. I enjoyed the personality.'

The Wednesday session began at 11am and 28 minutes later Montoya was quickest (221.566). At 11.57 the rain came, washing the rest of the day away. Montoya was expansive, answering questions on a wide variety of topics. On the IRL cars he said 'I think you have to make them better handling-wise. They're a bit different [from CART]. They're pretty simple to drive. They're a bit slower to react, and momentum is impor-tant. It would be very exciting to drive the CART cars here because we wouldn't be talking about 220, we'd be talking about 230s or 240s. It would be really fast.'

Vasser, whose career stretched back to before the split, knew the Speedway and advised Montoya that he'd find it easy. He did. 'It only took me four laps to do 217.'

He explained that although he didn't know the other drivers 'it won't take long to realise who's aggressive and who you can run side-by-side with.' Someone suggested he didn't seem intimidated by any racetrack.

Triumph at the
Indianapolis 500
the day after
Nazareth. The
front row (from
top): Greg Ray,
Montoya, Eliseo
Salazar. (IMS
Photo Operations)

'It's not about being intimidated. Some tracks you like more than others.'

The next CART round was Nazareth on Saturday, 27 May, one day before and 300 miles away from the 500. 'We're going to go out and run here. Not until the Thursday [before Nazareth] will we think about this. You don't have to be first in the first corner to win here. You just have to cruise for 400 miles and then race. I think it's going to be really exciting. We're going to be coming straight from Nazareth, which is a very small place. And when we come here I'm sure it will be like "whew, Jesus."' Later he'd add that 'being on ovals, it should be OK. If it were a road course for 500 miles it would be hard. Sometimes you test for a full day, so I don't think it will be that bad.'

On Thursday 18 May he went fastest (217.634) on his sixth lap ten minutes into the session, and quickest again at 4.55 (221.307) before Vasser, making a strong late run, did 221.681. Next day 47 cars took to the track at various times and Montoya finished seventh quickest (222.551). 'We were trying some things, and we made some gains on the car. It was just a little bit but we're comfortable where we are at.'

On Saturday 20 May he was fifth fastest in pre-quali-fying practice. Qualifying itself is utterly dissimilar to Formula 1: the drivers go one at a time, cover four laps and the average speed governs their grid position.

'Oval racing is a little bit different because you can gain so much from a draft,' Greg Ray explains. 'So to be really fair, to get the best driver in the best car – the person who's willing to lay it on the line the most – there is no drafting. Of course weather conditions can change and that part is not fair but otherwise it is. At Indy the historic picture – the unique tradition – is deep and the rules don't apply to any other racing, certainly that I've done. In road racing the best single lap that you can do places you on the grid. On ovals it's still only one lap. But at Indy it's a four-lap average and that makes it even more difficult, because there's a lot of people can throw in a quick one, then can't recover from it and maintain it.

'The press had quoted Montoya as saying "it's a piece of cake, it's easy" and it is easy as long as you're below the threshold. When you go to the edge in a racing car

– whether it's a Formula 1 car, an Indy Racing League car, a NASCAR, a Le Mans car – it's the same. Your job and the team's job is to get to the edge of adhesion with the equipment and push-push-push it. In 2000 it was all about how brave you were and how much downforce can you take off the car, how much dare you run without?[1] At Indy there are no rules. You can do what you want to do. And qualifying is outright pace – a different event: not a racing event, a speed event.'

Eliseo Salazar, a Chilean with A.J. Foyt Racing, did 223.231 just after midday. There was a tangible sense of anticipation – almost drama – as Montoya, starting at 1.19, did 223.636, 223.380, 223.236 and 223.236 again for an average 223.372. That took care of Salazar. The crowd delighted in what Montoya had just done.

'Two years ago,' Montoya said, 'after I signed to drive with Chip, the first time I came here it was a cold and windy day. And snowy. Typically Indy. I went through the museum and around the track. When the bus made the turn onto the straightaway I said "Geez, where's the other end?" It's so big. [Before now] I haven't experienced the track and the fans. Every single fan has been really good, and the drivers and teams also. When you've watched this race all these years, then you come here and see all the people, it's amazing.'

Greg Ray would go out at 3.49 that afternoon.

'It's hard to know for sure what the difference in the conditions were,' he says. 'The day, if I remember correctly, was cloudy and the air was getting thicker: more humidity so the air's thicker. The air creates a little more downforce but it also creates more drag and Indy is all about getting the right set up *and* getting rid of as much drag as you can. It is as delicate as that. You have to have the right springs, the right shocks, the right set-up, great motors...'

Presumably you could watch him qualifying.

'You can but what's the point? The car's going by at 240mph on the straightaway and there's four corners and you're not going to go out there to watch. Everybody's driving styles are different, and even wing settings and all those things are different. At Indy it looks easy until it comes time to have no downforce: you're still going 240mph down the straightaway surrounded by concrete walls, you're slippin' and slidin' and the

thing's moving around underneath you, and at that speed the walls look like one flat wall in *front* of you. It's a pretty daunting thing when you're on the edge, so you back up two, three miles an hour to put some downforce on the car. A pretty brilliant experience – but not fun. At 240 and looking at the flat wall, it's a very *real* experience and you have to make a very cognizant decision that could affect something permanently.'

Namely, your life.

Montoya would apparently be unfazed by Indy qualifying. But before we get to that, here is a brief explanation of the technical terminology. The wing on a racing car is to get air flowing over it, forcing the car down and giving it grip. Grip costs speed. If however you set the wing at a negative angle, it gives uplift and makes the car faster but at the cost of grip. The more negative the angle, the less grip: frightening. Or in mo-race speak, how big are your balls? Small adjustments (fractions of an inch) can be made by sliding a wicker – a spoiler – into a slot in the rear wing.

'Most of the cars had about zero degree rear wing and a lot of them ran an eighth or quarter inch wicker on the rear of the car,' Ray says. 'Some of the quicker cars qualified at negative one degrees. Montoya ran pretty easily about three degrees negative and an eighth inch wicker: that's the moment when it came down to it, when it was the "tale of the tape", when it's all about desire. We thought we had good motors that year and a horsepower advantage.' If you have a horsepower advantage, you can afford to trade a little more wing to gain grip.

The morning pre-qualifying practice session seemed to disprove that, because Montoya got into the top five (just) – and Ray didn't.

'We had to go to negative four – 4.2 or 4.3 – on the rear wing and we ran like a sixteenth wicker for less downforce. He was fully committed, I was fully committed, he was fully flat, I was fully flat, and we just had to take a little bit more off.'

You know what you've got to beat because he's already been.

'When I go out there I don't necessarily think of it in those terms,' Ray says. 'You know other cars are quick but you've got to be quicker. I can't remember when

The Indianapolis
Speedway was just
another racetrack
and the 500 miles
just another race,
OK? (Getty Images)

I've had a good car and *haven't* been flat at any racetrack. Never lift. Hustle through the corners, slipping and sliding, correcting. That goes for a place like Richmond, which is insane – we have gone as fast as 167mph average on a ¾ mile closed racetrack. At Indy, when the car's right for qualifying, you can always run flat. My mind set is: *Montoya's gone quick, we have to go quicker even though the conditions are pretty tough* – and getting worse because the air was getting thicker and thicker and more and more humid.'

At 3.49 Ray did 223.658, then 223.397, 223.503 and 223.325 for an average 223.471. Pole. He said 'the Man Upstairs was with me through every corner.'

Reflecting now, Ray says 'that's not much of a difference' – 223.471 against 223.372 – 'considering it's a two and a half mile track and so four laps is ten miles. That's pretty amazing. The biggest difference was the cars. I ran a Dallara and he ran a G-Force. I think everybody thought the mechanical package on the G-Force was a little bit better.

'I was flat and I knew the four laps were very, very close. I could have wiggled my elbows and that would have been the difference in the average speed for the whole thing! I was hanging it out: the car was really loose-loose-loose and I said that day I could hold my breath for 160 seconds because that's what I had to do! I was being facetious, of course, but it *was* tough. The 160 seconds? It's four laps of 40 seconds each and every time it gets hairy you've got to hold your breath to steady your body and steady your mind...'

And that was qualifying.

'Yes, we spoke after qualifying because between then and the race we'd had to do a couple of things together, some media stuff. He struck me as totally different out of the car. There was a time on the pit lane where I was walking by and he waved and said something. I couldn't hear him so I walked over and sat down on the wall next to him. We talked for a bit. His overall demeanour was of a young, carefree person but I wasn't offended by it. All I knew about him was what I'd read and seen on TV, and it's pretty much like anything else: he was very laid back, very funny, very jovial, never showed any signs of stress. He was easy to talk to, he was fun to talk to, clowning around a little bit for the cameras. I was very relaxed around him. We never got into heavy, deep, serious subjects. We talked about conditions or *hey, that was a handful*. We kind of paralleled it from our experiences but I never felt that

Easy does it at Indy. (LAT)

he was hiding anything or had a hidden agenda. Out of the race car he was just nice to talk to.'

They practised on Thursday 25 May and Montoya went quickest early on (162.075). That was no more than warming to his work and at 12.15 he was up to 218.257, a time that would not be bettered. 'I think I've got a good race car now.' And with that he went to Nazareth.

There he qualified on pole and led the first half of the race but damaged a tyre running over debris and damaged the nose of the car in a crash. He was thirteenth and forced his way to fourth by the end. He felt, as he had felt at Motegi, that the car was good enough to be a race winner. And with that he went to Indianapolis.

Sunday 28 May. The race ought to have started at 11am, but rain delayed that and the rolling start would finally come shortly after 2. During the delay Montoya said he was 'really trying to take it easy. Then we walked out and saw all the people. I looked at my girlfriend and said "Jesus, it's packed. This is unreal."' The crowd was 400,000.

Ray remembers 'talking to him right before we were going to get in the cars and again it was a very, very light conversation.'

One report[2] says Montoya was so laid-back before the start that he whistled as he sat in his car on the front row. Some quarter of an hour before the race began, he was gazing at a blonde wearing very little and said something that made her laugh. He gazed at Ray alongside him, his attention caught – maybe – by Greg pulling on his helmet. He gazed, now, at one of Ray's front tyres and then at the blonde again. While this was going on the crowd were booing him, loudly.

Yes, a CART man deep in the enemy's camp.

'I don't remember the crowd booing him,' Ray says. 'It's always more important when you've got to impress your peers than impress the public. The public sometimes has this childhood mentality about things. There was still rivalry between CART and IRL and Montoya at Indy was a foreigner in both senses of the word. Something of the statements he had made when he first tested there were purely candid and Indy was just another racetrack to him. He didn't grow up in America and he didn't have his heart set on Indy Car racing – he had his heart set on Formula 1 from a very early age. The press ran with some of the remarks he made in lots of articles and people read those. So if people were booing him that might be the explanation but I don't even think about that.'

Ray, of course, was isolating himself from everything except the race. Within a moment he would face a most unusual problem. He had a man he had never raced against alongside him on the front row and – going wheel to wheel at these high speeds – who knew how Montoya would behave? Ray has an intriguing philosophy about handling that.

'I knew he was aggressive in the racecar, no way different than I expected myself to be. But I didn't know if he was fair and aggressive. Finding out? We're all big boys. You learn to play within the rules that the people around you are playing by: one dirty move and all of a sudden you understand what the guy's about – and you may make life equally as difficult for him as he's just done for you.

'You approach one guy one way and another guy a completely different way. In Formula 1 in recent years there has been so little passing that the drivers really don't learn that – they learn how to block – but we pass each other so often you learn about the people you're passing.'

It is a matter of practical experience, which includes contradictions.

'When you look at somebody's face out of the car you may read a certain personality and you can anticipate the sort of replies they'll give to questions and the sort of remarks they'll make. Take that exact same person – who may be a total blank out on the street – and put him in a car. He plays it by the rules, fair, respectful, he'll make it hard on you but give way. Then you'll see another guy who's very jovial, personable, liked by everybody. You put him in a racecar and *he's* the biggest bastard you'll ever meet. You can't pass him and he's trying to kill you and basically he's trying to kill himself.'

Which was Montoya? Ray took as a form guide the 1999 crash between Montoya and Michael Andretti at Motegi where, Ray believes, 'Michael said to him *you can't use your car as a weapon*. I've had drivers that

A picture of tranquillity after the battle was won. Montoya and Chip Ganassi with the Indy 500 Trophy. (Getty Images)

I've had run-ins with and some people hold grudges for a lifetime. It was good that he and Montoya were able to deal with it' – encouraging, too, as the minutes ticked away to the 500 start.

'We'd practised together,' he says. 'Keep in mind that the 500 is a long event and you have plenty of time for practice. I hadn't witnessed anything or heard any remarks about Montoya but, yes, I didn't *know*.'

The final part of Ray's philosophy was utterly basic. 'In fact I didn't put a lot of thought into this – maybe it's my own arrogance that if I have a good car I don't care what he does. I have 500 miles to get it right: you can make life difficult for me but if my car's good, no problem. I was going to be cautious with him at first.'

At 2.03 the 33 cars rolled from the grid and began the parade lap. The Pace Car released them and Ray and Robby Gordon went wheel-to-wheel into Turn One, Ray emerging in front. Between Turns Three and Four Montoya went past Gordon. A classic motor racing duel was about to unfold and Ray took a 1.147 lead into lap two. The duel, however, would eventually be flawed. Ray knew that already.

'We didn't run nearly enough downforce and I think I could have got away with that problem but we had way too much balance to the back of the car, so the car *pushed* and on an oval you have to lift, and if you have to lift you're slow. There's no way around it, that's just the way it is. We ran gears that were way too long and in the race I never got out of fourth gear – couldn't use fifth or sixth. Well, I might have got into fifth a couple of times when I was drafting him...'

At lap 8 Ray led by 1.144 seconds. Gordon got past Montoya on lap 13 but they were lapping backmarkers and next lap Montoya retook him between Turns 3 and 4. At lap 15 Ray led him by 1.741. At lap 20 Ray led him by 1.070 but seven laps later Montoya took him on the inside of the front straight – four cars were running abreast. Ray struck back immediately, retaking Montoya in Turn One. Montoya immediately retook Ray. Montoya was almost on the grass.

'He was fast but he made a mistake,' Montoya would say. 'I passed him and I made the same mistake. He passed me. Then he made the mistake again and I passed him.' It was very, very intoxicating to watch for the 400,000, and never mind who was friend and who was enemy.

'We were fighting but he was being extremely honourable and fair,' Ray says. 'When I had a run on him he didn't try to block me at the last second or wiggle – it can happen that people have no intention of cutting you off but they kinda wiggle to make you think they might. He never did that, nor did I do that to him. He was clean. I was just disappointed that we didn't have the car to fight with him.'

At lap 27 Montoya passed Ray on the inside and became the forty-seventh driver to lead his first Indianapolis. A lap later Ray struck back and retook the lead.

'The first so many laps he and I traded places. We ran side-by-side a bunch, I would run in front for five or seven laps and he'd run in front for five or seven laps. We'd be in traffic and he'd catch me, then I'd get stuck in traffic and he'd pull out a 200 yard lead, then I'd get some open air and I'd catch him up. It was back and forth but I didn't have a car which would allow me to fight hard *with* him.'

An amusing anecdote, hereabouts. In the first rush of pit stops, Montoya was in and Vasser led. When Montoya emerged he came up behind Vasser and assumed he was lapping him. 'I called Chip and said "tell Jimmy to move over" and he said "uh, Juan, he's the *leader*. That's for position." And I said "oh..."'

A lap later Vasser peeled off into the pits for his stop and Montoya now led the race so comfortably that he said he was just having fun and began cracking jokes with the team over the radio. Someone[3] mischievously said that Montoya's car was so good and needed so little attention – apart, of course, from the usual refuelling and tyre changing – that 'the guys from the neighbourhood garage could have manned the pit.' Montoya reinforced that by explaining that the car was perfect and 'we didn't have to risk anything.'

At lap 50, the race settled after the first pit stops, Montoya led Gordon by 7.518 seconds, Ray now seventh. Five laps later Montoya had increased that lead to 21.866 seconds. The second pit stops started soon after and these brought the end for Ray.

'I was trying too hard and, because I was complaining every lap about the car pushing and the gears being too long, the only thing the team could figure out was to take more downforce off the car and try to rebalance it. I went out, cold tyres, 35 gallons of fuel, which is a lot of weight – and unfortunately the car slid into the dirty part of the racetrack. And if you get there you're in trouble. I bumped the wall in Turn Two and that was the end of my day. I enjoyed it, but keep in mind when I'm racing a car I don't care about those 400,000 people and I don't care who's in that other car. I'm a non-discriminatory driver: I want to kick everybody's ass. And that's the way all drivers are.'

At lap 85 Montoya led Vasser by 6.88 seconds, at lap 88 it was out to 9.24.

There was a beautiful control about his driving, an ease and a certainty which put you in mind of *The Thomas Crown Affair* film and its haunting background song, 'The Windmills Of Your Mind', and its lovely lines about a circle in a spiral, and an ever-spinning wheel.

A moment of threat came after a re-start on lap 161 when Buddy Lazier drew full up to Montoya and ducked out trying to get by. He fended that off.

Montoya pitted at lap 175 and now Vasser led. On

lap 180 Montoya took him at the entrance to Turn Three. He pulled steadily away so that at lap 191 his lead stood at 8.84 seconds. Lazier took Vasser on lap 193 and Montoya would confess that 'there were a few times I was worried when Lazier got close'.

He needn't have been. He won the race by some seven seconds.

He had led 167 of the 200 laps and become the first rookie to do that since Graham Hill in 1966. He said the most difficult aspect had been 'just keeping everything together. Trying to keep cool. You've got to keep aggressive. Every lap I had to keep pushing.'

Ganassi insisted that Montoya was 'the best driver in the world right now' and added that this was 'the biggest moment of my life'.

The race had been covered live on Colombian television and Bogotá went slightly wild. Evidently as Montoya crossed the line the commentator called him 'the monster of Colombian motor racing' – meaning it as a tribute. One report said that Montoya's wins, including this one, were bringing relief to the Colombian people, locked into the endless guerrilla war and a devastating economic recession. President Andres Pastrana was among those hypnotised by the TV coverage and spoke of the country's pride.

Greg Ray spoke to him at the awards banquet 'and he was the same as before, very jovial. His personality didn't change. My experience with Montoya was that I enjoyed it very much. I like aggressive people, I like people who say what's on their mind. I cannot stand people that are so politically correct that they sit on the fence and you never really get to know who they are. You draw a line in the sand and unless you cross it people don't know who you are and you don't know who they are. Montoya is aggressive in the racecar. So was I. He was a little bit arrogant at times with the media – haven't we all been?'

There's an amusing footnote, and although the two people quoted give slightly different versions, all the essentials match.

Robin Miller: 'Evidently there was a CART drivers' meeting after Montoya won the Indy 500 and I don't know if he was late or what but something happened. Andretti gave him a hard time about "the big Indy 500

winner" and Juan went "how many times you won it?" Michael's led 400 laps at Indy and never won the race.'

Mo Nunn: 'He and Michael are in a drivers' meeting and Juan had won the Indy 500. So Juan was sitting there and he said something which the other drivers didn't think maybe he should have said. Michael said something like "hark at Mr Big Shot now he's won the 500" and Montoya said something like "well, at least I did it first time, you've been trying 13 times and you ain't done it yet."'

That would have been Milwaukee, a race Montoya won from pole. Here he had to remind himself not to be too aggressive. Round about now, rumours – subsequently confirmed – suggested that Montoya would be joining Williams for 2001, replacing Jenson Button. (The confirmation came on 21 September, Williams saying that Montoya was 'being released with the blessing of Chip Ganassi.')

The CART season was not proving a success. At Detroit he led from pole but was halted by mechanical problems; at Portland he was fifth when the engine failed; at Cleveland he ought to have finished third but a late stop for fuel cost him places; at Toronto he and Franchitti crashed on the opening lap.

The finish of the Michigan race has rightly entered folklore. Gordon Kirby, a highly experienced observer of the motorsport scene, felt it might have been the greatest race of all – anywhere, anytime.

Friday, 21 July: 10.30 – the morning practice. Ten minutes in, Andretti was quickest (230.45mph), Montoya on 227.66. At 11.03 Montoya went fastest, 230.56. Four minutes later Castro-Neves went 231.44, at 11.10 Andretti went 234.16mph. At 11.40 Andretti burst through the track record with 235.47 but that was unofficial[4]. The session ended at midday: Montoya

outside the top ten, but the top 18 drivers separated by less than one second. The mood for the weekend had been established and, after a beautiful morning, that was reinforced at lunchtime when a bank of storm clouds rolled over.

Friday, 21 July: 2.0 – the afternoon practice. Ten minutes in, de Ferran was quickest with 232.55, Andretti third (228.58). At 2.20 Montoya was quickest (235.11) and that endured until 2.37 when Castro-Neves did 235.35. At 2.50 Tracy went quickest (236.74). The session finished at 2.59: Tracy, Andretti (235.47), Castro-Neves.

Saturday, 22 July: 8.0 – the morning practice. Five minutes in, Montoya had the fastest lap of the meeting so far (237.09) – and on only his fourth lap. It took until 8.40 for anyone to beat that: Tracy (236.71). Montoya responded with 237.24, and one minute later Andretti responded to *that* with 238.68. At 8.56, Tracy pushed that up to 238.93. Two minutes later Andretti responded to *that* with 238.68.

Saturday, 22 July: 11.0 – qualifying. Twenty minutes

in, Montoya was fourth quickest (232.53), but immediately Vasser went past (232.76). Andretti now produced 234.62 and – immediately – Tracy went past that (234.94). It was a new lap record. The session ended at 12.56 with Tracy on pole from Andretti, who said: 'The speeds just amazed me. We've got a good car for the race, we've just got to think "finish, finish, finish," and we'll be right there.'

Montoya was seventh…

Sunday, 23 July: 9.30 – final practice. Ten minutes in, Andretti was fastest (231.75), a speed eclipsed by de Ferran (231.96). Now 22 cars were within one second – but Montoya wasn't in the top ten. The talk, however, was of saving fuel and not worrying about position until near the end of the race. Andretti even said he had been ordered not to lead. The imperative was to get through the 250 laps (500 miles).

Sunday, 23 July: 1.45 – the race. The Pace Car begins to roll for the first of four laps holding the 24 racers behind it. At 1.50 the green flag was waved and the pack engulfed Tracy and Andretti. De Ferran dived

Well, this is
America. (Getty
Images)

towards the bottom of Turn One but Montoya and Andretti surged past. Montoya led the opening lap, Andretti behind him. The lead would change hands 52 times in terms of who led across the start-finish line and that involved ten drivers. The lead would change *162* times during the laps.

In précis: Montoya led lap two by 0.98 seconds from Andretti … on lap ten the gap was .247… on lap 22 Castro-Neves took the lead … at lap 50 it was Kenny Brack, Fittipaldi, Montoya … on lap 57 Montoya took the lead from Brack. Brack got that back and at lap 60 Montoya ran second, Andretti third … on lap 62 Andretti led … on lap 70 the order had become Andretti, Castro-Neves, Montoya … on lap 88 Papis, Castro-Neves, Brack, Fittipaldi, Montoya. You get the idea.

On lap 222, the yellow flag was out because Fittipaldi 'spins off on the backstretch, taking a wild ride through the infield grass before coming to stop at the bottom of Turn Three.'[5] This yellow lasted until lap 228 and, by touring slowly for the six laps, the drivers saved enough fuel to allow them to blast their way to the finish, 22 laps away.

By lap 230 Andretti was leading, Montoya seventh, but by lap 233 Montoya was up to second. Between laps 234 and 237 Montoya launched a sustained attack and got ahead *eight* times – but each time Andretti held him. On lap 238 Montoya – finally – got by, but two laps later Andretti was back in the lead. As the race moved to its climax, Franchitti and Max Papis were not far behind the duel in front – and were themselves duelling. Cumulatively it brought the crowd to their feet and they'd stay there.

Lap 240: Andretti leads Montoya by .001 of a second.
Lap 245: Andretti leads Montoya by .003 of a second.
Lap 246: Andretti leads Montoya by .010 of a second across the line, but into Turn One Montoya 'slides past'.
Lap 247: Montoya leads Andretti by .193 of a second.
Lap 248: Montoya leads Andretti by .216 of a second.
Lap 249: Andretti re-takes the lead at Turn Three. They move into the last lap.

'It was a drafting race,' Andretti says. 'The way we set up the wings and stuff, it was for the last dash – the last 20 laps. It just so happened that it came down to myself and Juan and we traded the lead probably 20 or

30 times in that 20 laps. It went back to Motegi: we could trust ourselves to put on a performance like that. I trusted him and he trusted me. We ran wheel-to-wheel just about touching, but not touching, for 20 laps and it was going back and forth, back and forth. It was just good – great – clean racing.

'We're talking about speeds in the 230mph range and when I say close I mean, literally, inches: *almost* touching. You don't really look over at the other guy, you see each other out of your peripheral vision. You know that you're very close to him and basically it was a chess game which came down to the last lap.'

Andretti was *thinking* like a chess player.

'Everything went perfectly for me. Juan actually took the bait – took the lead into Turn One but I knew I was going to be able to get a run on him into Turn Three. I did.' If Andretti got by, that might leave Montoya no time to respond. If Andretti got by…

Into Turn Three, Andretti pulled level with and below Montoya.

It ought to have been checkmate.

'The biggest problem,' Andretti says, 'was a lapped car in front of me' – Tarso Marques in a Swift-Ford. 'If the lapped car would just have gone down to the inside I'd have gotten his draft and he would have pulled me ahead of Juan, but instead he went wide and pulled Juan – that's how Juan beat me. If that lapped car hadn't been there…'

Montoya had seen Marques ten laps from the end but 'I didn't think we'd catch him, then he got closer, closer, closer.'

Andretti and Montoya side-by-side: they faced a blast through Three and Turn Four to the line. They were coming at Marques like the wind. Out of Four – hammer-hammer-hammer – one report (Kirby) says Andretti and Montoya touched briefly: marks on their cars proved this. The official CART report says 'Andretti stays way below Montoya all the way to Turn Four. The cars touch wheel-to-wheel coming to the flag.' Andretti is sure they didn't touch…

Out of Turn Four, Montoya surveyed Marques and thought I'm not going to lift. If *I'm going to have to hit the guy I'm going to hit him.*

Marques was on the right and moved a little bit

further right up towards the wall.

'I was almost *over* the wall trying to get away from them,' Marques would say. 'I tried to stay very close to the wall because I didn't want to change the result of the race.'

Now Marques was directly ahead of Montoya and – briefly but crucially – towing him as they reached towards the line. It was enough. Montoya crossed the line .040 of a second before Andretti: less than the length of a car. It was the third closest finish in CART history.[6]

This is what they said then.

Andretti: 'It was a little bit of stupid racing out there for a while because we had to try and make it on one more pit stop and everybody was just backing off. Nobody wanted to lead: if you did, you were burning more fuel and towing everybody else, and it was a bit of a joke. We were all just backing off. You'd have thought we were shooting a movie or something the way it was going – but it was all basically setting it up for the end, the shoot-out, and when that yellow came out it was really perfect for a shootout because we weren't going to have to conserve fuel.

'It came down to the last ten laps, so I knew it was going to be very important to try to get away from the rest of the group. Then it came down to Juan and myself working together, and I think we both knew that we both needed to break away, so we really worked together where we were leap-frogging away from the rest of the pack. We knew then that it was going to be between the two of us, so with about two laps to go I saw that they [the pack] weren't going to be able to catch us and I really concentrated on just setting it up for the last turn. I was able to get him to do exactly what I wanted. I allowed him to go by into Turn One and I knew I wanted to get a draft going into Turn Three on him and get a run. I came off Turn Four really strong, in fact I pulled him a little bit because we were behind Tarso as well. I thought Tarso was actually going to help me because normally his line has been down low, but for some reason he decided to stay high. I got a little tow from him initially and then all of a sudden he went really up by the wall. I started fighting for that tow, and

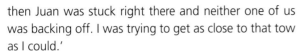

then Juan was stuck right there and neither one of us was backing off. I was trying to get as close to that tow as I could.'

Andretti now, reflecting: 'It was unfortunate because the whole race Tarso Marques was going down low but that time he decided to go high and he decided the outcome of the race. I wish he hadn't been there because then I think it would have come down to the good strategy that we had and we'd have been able to win – by a nose…'

Montoya: 'Before the last caution [yellow] I was behind Michael, I was pretty fast and I thought he was going to have to save fuel – but he didn't. I was a little disappointed in that, but then the yellow came out and, after that, we were neck-and-neck. I didn't know what was going to happen. He pushed me up the track[7] coming off the last turn, then the backmarker moved up a little bit and I got a little tow. I didn't think I had a chance to win this race, but then I jumped from seventh to first at the start and I thought *this is pretty good*.[8]

A footnote from Miller. 'After the Michigan 500, when they banged wheels, Montoya was funny because three or four days later he says "why would a guy with all the money Michael Andretti's got, as old as he is, be driving that hard? What's wrong with that guy?" He was laughing. Then he said "I don't particularly like the guy but I do admire him driving that hard at 39 years of age."'

This, and the Indy 500, were beacons in a season largely of shadows. 'The Indianapolis win was big because there is so much tradition,' Montoya would say at Michigan, 'but I had a lot more fun here. First place, second, first, second – every quarter of a mile was exciting.'

At Chicago, Montoya had pole but a mechanical problem halted him; at Lexington a mechanical problem halted him after a spin; at Elkhart Lake yet another mechanical problem halted him. This, of course, did not reflect on his natural ability.

As Miller says: 'He had a couple of amazing races. He was leading at Portland and he spun coming out of the last turn, on his own, and he straightened it out so fast he barely lost any time. He was leading at Elkhart Lake and the gearbox seized, locked the rear tyres and

sent him into a spin – and he caught it, made the corner.'

Somehow, in this fraught season, the championship had never seemed a real possibility. After Elkhart Lake, Andretti led with 125 points from Roberto Moreno (112), Montoya ninth on 77.

Meanwhile in Formula 1, as David Sears recounts, Jenson Button was doing 'a good job in the Williams. Juan Pablo worried that he was going to push him out and that he was never coming back from America. In fact at one point he said to me "David, tell Frank I'll drive for nothing." I said "you don't ever tell Frank that because he'll say *great!*"'

At Vancouver – guess: mechanical problem after 67 laps; at Laguna Seca he ran second but an air jack failed at a pit stop and the team had to do it by hand. That made him sixth. 'I was disappointed but things like that are out of your control, so you can't get too frustrated.'

At Gateway, St. Louis, he won after Andretti suffered an engine failure. 'We've given away a lot of races. It's nice that someone gave one to me.'

Miller explains that despite Montoya's comparative lack of experience in CART 'he had such amazing car control. At St. Louis on an oval he carried an in-car camera so you could see. He probably "crashed" 15 times during the race but he never hit the wall – he kept saving it.'

At Houston he finished second behind Vasser after banging wheels with Castro-Neves and describing him as a 'nightmare'. At Surfers Paradise he took pole but crashed at the start with de Ferran. At Fontana, the last race, he finished tenth. He was ninth in the championship.

Miller insists that 'some of the best drives he made were in 2000 when the Lola wasn't very good compared to the Reynard and he just drove the wheels off. How he kept it on the course sometimes was amazing. He was so much fun to watch driving a racecar. There's an expression in the United States, *someone's got iced water in his veins*. And that's how he drives: take no prisoners. Don't give a damn. Don't be intimidated by anybody or anything. He was no more intimidated by Michael Andretti than he would be by Michael Schumacher….'

Before we move on, here is the overview of Montoya's career with Target Chip Ganassi by the team's Managing Director, Mike Hull.

'My favourite memory of Juan's championship year was the domination he showed on the track, but equally his enthusiasm to drive race cars – which is amazing. He wants to drive race cars and he wants to win. You can see that in his eyes when he gets to the track.

'His ability to dominate the race was also my favourite memory of his win in the Indy 500. He understood the race he had to run and the pace he needed to set. He was in control of that race from beginning to end.

'He appeared laid back – because he was! He was confident in his ability as a driver and the main reason for that was his mental preparation. He was able to mentally rehearse situations that he would encounter during a race. He appears unflappable because he has already gone over those situations in his mind. He's the best that I've seen at that: Juan rehearsed everything.

'Juan was a World Champion when he raced here, people just didn't know that yet. Americans were lucky to see such a talented driver. It's hard to compare drivers from different eras but in my opinion he's certainly one of the best ever.

'Out of the car, he's a great guy. He enjoys life and loves to have fun.'

That just about sums it all up.

NOTES

1. Downforce, by definition, gives the car adhesion but, also by definition, adhesion = suction = slowing the car.
2. ESPN International Ventures.
3. Ibid.
4. Unofficial: the official lap record could only be set in qualifying or the race.
5. CART news release.
6. The closest finishes up to then: Mark Blundell over de Ferran (0.027), Portland, 1997; Kanaan over Montoya (0.032), Michigan, 1999; Montoya over Andretti (0.040), Michigan, 2000; Unser Jnr over Scott Goodyear (0.043), Indianapolis, 1992; Pruett over Unser Jnr (0.056), Michigan, 1995.
7. Pushed – not physically but, rather, forcing him to go there.
8. CART news release.

It's a bit like this and a bit like that. Montoya talks to Ganassi lead engineer Bill Pappas at Laguna Seca, where he finished sixth. (Getty Images)

It's 2001 and Montoya will excite the whole of Formula 1 with Williams – and prove a problem to each of the Schumacher brothers. (Getty Images)

take that

The announcement that Montoya would be leaving Ganassi and joining Williams in Formula 1 was made in September 2000. Jenson Button, who had partnered Ralf Schumacher that season, would move to Benetton, with Williams retaining an option on him.

Montoya was 'much more ready to come back,' David Sears says, after the CART championship and Indy 500 in the States. He'd been 'terrible with the media out there' at the start but got much better at it. 'Some people now say he can be quite amusing but then he would spout some horrible bloody replies.' Formula 1, so insistent on manicured imagery, would not tolerate the curt or the uncouth.

Grand Prix racing is obsessed with its own seriousness, and Montoya would now find himself drawn into that. How he'd react was one intriguing aspect among many, because few drivers had come to Formula 1 with such a reputation and fewer still brought with them such a degree of anticipation.

Before we reach the seriousness, two gentle examples of Montoya's thinking.

The first is from Peter Argetsinger of Barber Saab, who wasn't surprised at the swift impact Montoya would make. 'I was telling people when he was still doing Formula 3000 *he'll end up being a World Champion.* I went to most of the CART races because Barber Dodge supports them. He and his father invited me to come to all the Grands Prix [in 2001] – but I have two kids and a mortgage, I have a job and I have to work! Pablo said "you believed in Juan

from the beginning and we really appreciate everything you did to help us." They are such warm, nice people.'

The second example is from the journalist Robin Miller. Because Montoya was leaving America for Williams, Miller 'talked to him all the time about women and Formula 1 and American culture. I said "when you go over there you've got an opportunity to have a different woman at every Formula 1 track, and you'll be our hero!"'

North American racing is more of a small family while Formula 1 represents not just the championship of the world but the limits of technology, colossal finance and all the rest. To Miller, that Montoya could join this, master it *and* seduce a succession of beautiful girls – thus proving the virility of North American racing – seemed a delicious anticipation in itself.

In the autumn of Montoya's first Williams season, the North Americans came to the new Midlands circuit of Rockingham for the seventeenth round of the CART championship. Rockingham did not clash with a Grand Prix and Montoya went there to visit. Miller had not forgotten about the girl in every pit: 'Montoya's walking around holding hands with Connie, the girl he's going to marry. 'I said "what's wrong with you?!" and he said [grinning broadly] "leave me alone!"'

Miller understood what the seriousness of Formula 1 could do. He had Alessandro Zanardi and Michael Andretti in mind: Zanardi came to Williams in 1999 from Ganassi, as the reigning CART champion. He endured a desperate season, scoring not one point.

Andretti, a former Indy Car champion, came to McLaren in 1993 from Newman/Haas and, partnering Senna, had a frustrating season, scoring only seven points.

'I think,' Miller says, 'that the Formula 1 mentality affected Alex Zanardi. Alex is a very upbeat, emotional guy who really responded to positive reinforcement – which you don't get a lot of in Formula 1. Michael Andretti picked a bad time to go. Senna was Michael's best ally in that whole deal because it wasn't a very good car. I tell you what, Michael had some really good runs and the only time they went testing during the season he was just a tenth behind Senna. Michael had the ability to do it.

'Montoya is so great for Formula 1 because nobody is going to play a mind game with him. It'll be the opposite. He can play mind games with them. He had Ralf Schumacher talking to himself! I've never even met Ralf Schumacher but I've been watching what Montoya says and he's been kicking that guy's ass – and you don't think that guy's thinking about it? Who else would say something like "well, put Schumacher in a Minardi and see how he does"? Montoya says that all the time. It's mischievous but that's what good about him."'

I'd mentioned to Paul Stewart that several people in this book likened Montoya to Senna. 'It's not a comparison I would make. They are completely different in temperament. It's a natural thing to make the comparison though. People might say "he looks like he could be the next Senna, he's *like* a Senna." I never saw it that way. I thought *he's Juan Pablo and he's going to be all right*.'

Richard Dutton was another who had no doubts about Montoya and Formula 1. 'Montoya was born with a talent, a natural talent, and then it's channelled. Some drivers come through and you just know they are special. We tested Jenson Button in Formula 3000 at the end of 1999 and he was too. You could tell. Give Montoya a car equal to Michael Schumacher's and, in my opinion, he'd become the best. If Montoya and Michael were in the same team, Montoya's mental strength would eventually take him to being the better of the two. In *his* mind, nobody has the ability he has.'

This is a powerful testament and one that demands expansion because the anticipation generated by Montoya's arrival was straightforward: could he take on Michael Schumacher and, in doing that, revive the excitement of Grand Prix racing? Consider. Although Mika Häkkinen took the world title in 1998 and 1999, the '99 championship was inherited because Schumacher broke his leg at Silverstone and Häkkinen only won from Eddie Irvine in the other Ferrari by two points.

Schumacher dominated 2000 with nine poles, nine wins and 108 points; nor could anyone doubt that this was the *beginning* of a much more extensive domination by him and Ferrari. They were gathering an

M-power meets
BMW-power
at last . . .
(Getty Images)

. . . but the 2001
season proved
to be very
frustrating. (LAT)

awesome strength by the moment. None of the current drivers – including Häkkinen and Schumacher's brother Ralf – could do much except follow the Ferrari, certainly over the duration of a season. Montoya might…

Before the first race of 2001, the Australian Grand Prix at Melbourne, Montoya took part in a question and answer session, and here are extracts from that.

What are the main differences between CART cars and Formula 1?

'These cars are a lot different to what I'm used to. It's in the incredibly fast corners – they're pretty wild and pretty exciting in an F1 car. The immediate difference I have noticed is that you have to be a lot smoother and smarter driving F1 cars. You can throw them around more than the ones I've been driving in America, but they are not as forgiving.

'My tests over the winter have been quite positive. Mostly if you consider that when I drove for the first time in Jerez last December nearly two years had gone since the previous time I sat in an F1 car. Anyway, I know what F1 is about and I have been to a lot of races in the past so it doesn't make me too apprehensive.'

What are your expectations for this first season?

'This is going to be a huge challenge for me, I don't know what to expect. I have to learn from other people and play it really smart. It's a learning year and although you want to try and win all the time, some-

times you don't have the car to be able to do that – as happened to me last year in America. The only thing I know is that I am going to go out there and give 100 per cent. It may take a year to win, maybe another year – or maybe three years – but when the time comes you have to be ready for it. Winning is not easy and even in Champ Cars [another name for CART] I never expected to win in my first year.'

What's your feeling about replacing Jenson Button?

'I was surprised when Frank Williams chose me ahead of Button. Jenson did a great job in his first year and I thought with a second season in the team it would have been even better with him. Obviously I liked Frank's decision and I hope I can live up to what is expected of me. When I first went into Indy Cars I replaced Alex Zanardi who had done really well in the series, so I see no problems. I don't really know what happened to Alex in F1. I watched him on TV and he was struggling, but that's not going to happen to me.

'I went to America not to be another Zanardi, and I am here in F1 to be myself, not another Button. I don't feel any pressure to match his results, not at all.'

How about Ralf, your new team-mate?

'It's important for us to have a good relationship because that is going to help the team. If everything works well together then it will improve faster than if there is fighting. Ralf is quick, which is really good

because we will push each other. In a team where there's no 1 and 2 driver, each must gain the respect through his results and the team is giving Ralf and myself exactly the same opportunities. I think a lot of the so-called problems came from the press claiming that he said this and I said that. I am sure we'll get on well.'

These last words are the sort which drivers say when they are on their best behaviour and tape recorders are turning. Like proclamations from politicians, they should be treated with caution. A driver must establish dominion over his team-mate, who will be trying to exert the same pressure on him: some teams believe that creative *dis*harmony is an excellent way to keep their drivers at 100 per cent all the time. It can be a rough old trade, this Formula 1.

Montoya had never driven Melbourne before, which he felt put him at a disadvantage. 'I have worked hard on digesting past telemetry and, combined with on-

board footage from last year, there's little else I can use in preparation. I will make the best use I can of Friday free practice and we'll go from there.'

Because Montoya was exploring Grand Prix racing, I propose to join him on his journey, race by race. Given the nature of the man, and the nature of the racing, it'll be quite a ride. For uniformity, I have structured the race descriptions in the same way with, wherever relevant, what Montoya said at the time; for simplicity I refer to Michael Schumacher as Schumacher and Ralf Schumacher as Ralf.

Australia, Melbourne. After free practice Montoya said 'I've been struggling a bit with the set-up of the car…but I've done some learning.' He was fifteenth. In qualifying he was 'very disappointed' with his last run – baulked, as he claimed, by a slower car. That was the sixth row of the grid. Quite a ride? Remember that Montoya hadn't been in a standing start to a race since

1998 (in Formula 3000). Also that he did not feel in 'awe' (his word) of any of the other drivers on that grid, Schumacher included. He would have felt this awe if Senna had been there, but was so relaxed he surprised himself.

At the lights Montoya was reportedly caught by surprise but set off with ferocious acceleration, placing the car mid-track and almost touching a Jordan on the run down to Turn One, a right-hander. There he braked too late, went onto the grass and came back on again like the wind. At Turn Three, another right-hander, he went in line astern with Irvine (Jaguar) and both went off. Quoth Irvine: 'Montoya tried to overtake me from a long way back and knocked me off, but there will be no repercussions.'

Montoya came back like the wind again and, late on, got himself as high as third during the final flurry of pit stops before the engine blew up. He'd set fourth fastest lap and decided 'Formula 1 can be fun'.

Incidentally, Heidfeld – now with Sauber – hadn't seen Montoya 'for a long time after our Formula 3000 season, until Formula 1, in fact. I think he is doing a good job in Formula 1. He's quick, as I expected. During the Formula 3000 season we had had some problems and we'd had a fight: it was not like when the races were over we became the best of friends – there was still a lot of tension. Now I get along with him a lot better and we have no problems at all.'

Malaysia, Sepang. Another unknown circuit although he'd driven 'many' laps of it on video games and watched 2000 on-board footage. In free practice 'it looked like every problem was falling on me. First a fuel problem, then an electrical problem.' The only consolation was that the track itself didn't seem as much of a problem as, unseen, it had. In qualifying he was up to sixth but spun in the race on lap 4. A deluge engulfed the circuit and he'd been aquaplaning. Everybody else had too.

Brazil, Interlagos. Before he set off for Sao Paulo he said 'this week I had one day of testing in Barcelona and now I'm spending a couple of days in Madrid with my girlfriend. I need to recover because I am still a bit jet-lagged. In the morning I am waking at 5. Before I fly to Sao Paulo I'll spend a few days in Colombia.' Interlagos was the third new track: in CART he'd raced at Rio.

In free practice he was fourth, the first really significant moment of his Grand Prix career. He was moving towards the pace, and qualified fourth too. At the lights, Häkkinen stalled and Montoya swept round him, tucking in behind Schumacher. As the cars travelled round this opening lap the Safety Car came out because Häkkinen 's McLaren had not yet been moved from the grid. That allowed Montoya to draw up to Schumacher. The Safety Car peeled off, releasing the racers.

Montoya thought *this could be good.*

They moved towards the first corner, the corkscrew left-right. Montoya had spent the last two years of his life dealing with precisely such rolling starts as this.

Montoya thought *the Ferraris have more drag than we do, making Schumacher slightly slower.*

He was catching Schumacher who positioned the Ferrari full to the right approaching the corkscrew.

Montoya thought *I'll go inside and I know how late I can brake. If he brakes later, he's got the corner. If he doesn't…*

Schumacher came across towards him, feeling for the racing line, as they both turned in. Halfway round the left of the corkscrew Schumacher was squeezing Montoya hard, forcing him further and further to the inside – and Montoya was not yet level with him.

The F1 career started with a bang – he had Eddie Irvine off on the first lap in Australia just moments after this. (LAT)

Montoya stayed there, conceding nothing. This was the essence of the man: he knew some people would describe what he was doing as 'brave' but it wasn't that at all. To Montoya, Schumacher was just another guy to be beaten.

The unfolding of the corner carried Schumacher to mid-track, Montoya following him there and now hemming *him*. They nudged, Schumacher forced to put two wheels on the grass as they reached towards the right of the corkscrew. That left Montoya free and he accelerated. It had been one of the great overtaking moves in both a physical and psychological context, and it was more than that. Here was one of those pivotal moments when a new generation challenges the established order – and wins.

It scarcely matters that Montoya shed Schumacher quickly, nor that on lap 39 Jos Verstappen (Arrows) ran into the back of the Williams after Montoya had lapped him.

The great gesture had been made.

'I had a really healthy lead,' he said, 'and we were looking strong for a race win here.' Although journalists and TV interviewers hemmed him now – the race still going on in the background – he appeared calm, ordinary, matter-of-fact. 'I'm a bit disappointed that we didn't really get it.' He rolled his big eyes and seemed very young then. 'But I'm still happy for BMW, Williams and Michelin. They really did a fantastic job and I just want to thank everybody.'

It was authentic driver-speak. More authentically, he relegated the overtaking move to these words: 'I pushed it and that was it. No one is invincible.'[1] Those words were more powerful because, as he insisted, he was a racer and wasn't making much of what he had done. *Hey, guys, what's all this fuss?*

Mo Nunn, so wise in the ways of motorsport, puts The

The move which astonished Formula 1: Montoya elbows Schumacher aside at Sao Paulo. (LAT)

Move into a broader context. 'His dad came to me and said "Morris, do you think Juan will be OK in Formula 1?" and I said "don't even worry about it. He has the character." It was not a surprise to me at Sao Paulo when he went up the inside of Schumacher. He was there to show him *I'm not afraid of you*. In a way that was what he'd done to Andretti [at Motegi in 1999].

'What happens with these guys is this: Montoya's behind, he's shown that kind of aggression and that he intends to get to the top. That has a big effect psychologically on other drivers. When they look in the mirror and they see Schumacher coming or Montoya coming they get out of the way. They'll move because they think: *this guy's going to try and get past no matter what*. There are other drivers that will come up, stay behind and never make the attempt – and you don't give way to them.'

Before Imola, Montoya expanded on The Move. 'Initially when I passed him I was surprised because I was a long way back when we got to the braking. I said *just give it a try* and it worked, really. It was good. When I passed him I thought he should be a lot quicker than me and he would try to pass me fairly. I paced myself to a decent pace but I wasn't pushing really hard. I was trying to do clean running and take care of the tyres because we were on one stint. We were going to go a long way so I didn't want to try to get in front of Michael Schumacher and kill the tyres after ten laps. After I settled in I started pushing harder to see how fast he could run and I actually started pulling away from him. I couldn't believe it. I went *wow, I am going faster!*

'I think passing Schumacher was a good move but there have always been moves better than this that maybe people have never seen on TV. The pressure on me is big because I passed Michael, and what he is for the people is huge. He knows what he is doing and has a lot of experience, but I think what my move shows is that there can be some drivers capable of beating Michael. I always push, push really hard and I am not keen on giving anything away…'

He was asked – almost a philosophical question – about how much frustration he must have felt over Verstappen taking him out.

'No, that is racing. It is the same as if there's a technical problem with the car. If this happens, I am not going to kick the car and kick everybody in the team! That is where you have got to learn to be on top of your game. I was so happy with the job I had done that being put out of the race was disappointing, but it was another step forward for me. If I had won ten races I would be livid if that happens, I would go ballistic, believe me, and going ballistic was something I used to do in the past. At this point I am just moving forward, learning more and trying more and getting further. I remember when I got out of the car I could hear the fans screaming and I lifted my hand and waved to them and they went crazy and I felt really good because I knew I had done a good job. I didn't cock it up, I didn't spoil it, I didn't do anything silly, so I was very pleased with that.'

He added that Frank Williams and Patrick Head were 'pretty pleased because it was a big emotional moment for Williams Fl, and I would include myself as part of the team's family. You know for Williams Fl since 1997 they have not been up at the front and it was just like the team had opened the door. Being up there is not only me, it is everybody.'

San Marino, Imola. He'd raced here in Formula 3000 but said 'my race lasted about five laps before I crashed'. He had a difficult free practice, twenty-second, and qualified seventh. In the race he was running fifth when, at his second pit stop, he couldn't get 'any more gears'.

Spain, Barcelona. He knew this circuit intimately, with the Formula 3000 victory in 1998 and all the Formula 1 testing. In free practice he couldn't 'get a handle on the car' trying to set it up and was thirteenth. Qualifying was frustrating, with traffic and a yellow flag. From twelfth place on the grid he finished the race second, but more than half a minute behind Schumacher. He said he hadn't expected to be on the podium because 'the car was quite tricky to drive, and McLaren and Ferrari were in a different league'.

Austria, A1-Ring. He'd raced here twice in Formula 3000 and now in free practice was eleventh. He qualified second and might have improved on that but 'the wind changed direction to a head wind' after his second run. Schumacher had pole. It was tight: 1m 09.562

Locking horns in Austria, where in another muscular manoeuvre he wouldn't yield to Schumacher. (LAT)

against Montoya's 1m 09.686. Montoya seized the lead in the race but Schumacher tracked him and they arm-wrestled, Montoya conceding nothing. In a corner Montoya braked late, locked up and ran wide forcing Schumacher to run wide with him. They both went into the gravel trap. Montoya described it as a 'racing incident', Schumacher said Montoya hadn't been looking where he was going. Ultimately the Williams lost hydraulic pressure.

Monaco, Monte Carlo. He was tenth in free practice, seventh in qualifying, ran fifth in the race and crashed. 'I made a mistake and paid for it. The car was good and I have nothing to complain about. My accident happened when I shifted down, had understeer and went into the barrier.' This was near the swimming pool.

Canada, Montreal. Another new track which he'd find 'pretty interesting. You have got to be gentle with the car – it is quite good fun.' He qualified tenth and retired from the race after 20 laps. 'It was really strange because when I went over the kerb and put the power on, the rear just stepped out. I don't know what happened. I was doing exactly the same thing every lap.'

Europe, Nürburgring. Another track he knew from 3000, he qualified third and finished the race behind Schumacher, the winner, but much closer: 4.217

seconds. It was a restrained drive. Initially Ralf put the pressure on Schumacher but a ten second stop/go penalty took him from the equation. Montoya, with a 'competitive' car, decided to 'pick up the pace slowly' with the Schumachers ahead. 'The car was very positive and there was room in it to go quicker when I needed it.'

France, Magny-Cours. He'd never raced here, although he had tested in 1998 and one day this season. He qualified sixth, raced to lap 53 and 'the engine just died.'

Britain, Silverstone. Familiar ground because he'd raced on both the full and National circuits. He qualified eighth, despite clipping the kerb on the exit to Becketts and having to take the T-car, which was set up for Ralf. He finished the race fourth.

Germany, Hockenheim. The power of BMW came into full play and pole lay between Montoya and Ralf. Just before the mid-point Ralf had it with a 1m 38.458 and increased that ten minutes later to 1m 38.136. With 17 minutes left, Montoya put together 1m 38.117. 'Ralf ran me pretty close, he did four runs, I did three and my second one went so well.' He led the race and 'up to the pit stop it was going perfectly for me. We then had a problem with the refuelling rig and

this lost me the lead. I had a safe second place and two laps later the engine just went.'

Hungary, Budapest. He liked the Hungaroring but only qualified eighth. 'We try one thing and it makes the car have a big understeer, so we cure the understeer and then I can't turn in.' He finished eighth and said it was 'one of those weekends when nothing really worked for it. The car felt bad from the beginning to the end of the race but I was determined to finish because the boys had worked so hard for me. What can I say? Just a weekend to forget.'

Belgium, Spa. 'A great track.' He took pole in traditional wet-dry Spa weather. Both Schumachers were involved this time, Michael taking provisional pole (1m 57.271) and, four minutes later, increasing it (1m 56.921). Ralf and Montoya went head-to-head and in the final rush the team, thinking strategically, gave both enough fuel for two laps. Montoya did his first conservatively 'just to get on the grid' (1m 55.875),

and a moment later Ralf responded (1m 52.959). Montoya crossed the line just before the session ended and gave Spa the full treatment: 1m 52.072.

The race was traumatic. At the lights he stalled. There was a re-start, he was at the back of the grid and 'I went off like a rocket. I was looking good until de la Rosa ran into me. Then the car was pulling to one side and I was a bit scared something was going to break so on the first lap I took it quite easy. I was pushing pretty hard past three or four cars and passed Ralf. It was kind of exciting. Then the engine went.'

Italy, Monza. He likened it to Hockenheim in terms of power producing great speed and concluded that 'we should be really quick'. Free practice confirmed that, Ralf quickest – from Montoya. 'Today went from bad to better.' He turned that into pole, from Barrichello, Schumacher third, Ralf fourth. He said it felt 'pretty good' to beat the Ferraris and was asked (mischievously) if it felt as good as outqualifying Ralf at

Hockenheim? 'Yeah, better than that, even.' He won the race and, as races go, it was straightforward. 'At the beginning I had lots of oversteer everywhere, but the car got better and better and the speed was there when I needed it. I think this is a great day for me, especially as my father is here and it is his birthday.'

USA, Indianapolis. He qualified fourth and ran second behind Schumacher – at one point he had overtaken him – but was stopped by what he thought was hydraulic failure. It disappointed him because he thought he could have won.

Japan, Suzuka. He'd raced twice in Japan before but at Motegi, not Suzuka. He relished the prospect now because he'd heard the track was 'a proper racing circuit with great corners'. He was second in free practice ('the track is brilliant') and sustained that in qualifying, finishing the race second, 3.154 seconds behind Schumacher.

The championship: Schumacher 123, Coulthard 65,

The first win of Montoya's F1 career: Monza, 2001. From pole, he leads the Ferraris and Ralf as the race begins to develop.
(Getty Images)

He'd beat Barrichello by more than five seconds, with Ralf finishing third and Michael fourth. On the podium his delight is clear.
(Getty Images)

Barrichello 56, Ralf 49 and Montoya, sixth, on 31.

Because the relationship between team-mates is always a delicate and revealing one, here (in the blue tables below) are the respective performances of Ralf Schumacher and Montoya against each other. (DNF = Did Not Finish)

Even with a healthy scepticism about what statistics really prove, Ralf outqualified Montoya 11/6 in 2001. You can't tell much from the races because so many variables are in play, especially since the Williams cars failed to finish exactly half their starts, so which driver established superiority over the other would have to

The uneasy partnership, Montoya and Ralf Schumacher, each struggling for superiority (LAT), and statistics showing their comparative results.

2001	Qualifying		Race	
	RS	JPM	RS	JPM
Australia	5	11	DNF	DNF
Malaysia	3	6	5	DNF
Brazil	2	4	DNF	DNF
Imola	3	7	1	DNF
Spain	5	12	DNF	2
Austria	3	2	DNF	DNF
Monaco	5	7	DNF	DNF
Canada	2	10	1	DNF
Europe	2	3	4	2
France	1	6	2	DNF
Britain	10	8	DNF	4
Germany	2	1	1	DNF
Hungary	4	8	4	8
Belgium	2	1	7	DNF
Italy	4	1	3	1
USA	2	3	DNF	DNF
Japan	3	2	6	2

2002	Qualifying		Race	
	RS	JPM	RS	JPM
Australia	3	6	DNF	2
Malaysia	4	2	1	2
Brazil	3	1	2	5
Imola	3	4	3	4
Spain	3	4	11	2
Austria	2	4	4	3
Monaco	4	1	3	DNF
Canada	4	1	7	DNF
Europe	2	1	4	DNF
Britain	4	1	8	3
France	5	1	5	4
Germany	2	4	3	2
Hungary	3	4	3	11
Belgium	4	5	5	3
Italy	3	1	DNF	DNF
USA	5	4	16	4
Japan	5	6	DNF	4

M-power and BMW-power, at Imola, 2002. However hard he forced the Williams, there was no catching the Ferraris. (Getty Images)

wait to 2002. Montoya himself likened the relationship to working in an office – you don't have to like everybody there but you do have to work with them. In 2002, the qualifying which Ralf won 11/6 in 2001 would become 8/9, and of course Montoya would put together an astonishing five consecutive poles. Only Ralf won a race but Montoya would prove consistent and when it was necessary he could keep The Monster firmly under control.

A footnote to the 2001 season, from Peter Dumbreck. 'When we'd driven against each other I got to know him a little bit. I wouldn't call him one of my best mates. When I saw him at the *Autosport* awards in December he recognised me and came straight over. It's good to know that people like that don't change.'

Now Montoya faced his second Formula 1 season.

Australia, Melbourne. He said, untypically, 'I didn't really fancy racing at Melbourne for the first time last year but once I got the hang of it, it was a pretty good place to compete.' He qualified sixth in a rainy session and, as the race settled, he duelled with Schumacher, overtook him. 'I had a pretty good battle with Michael and when I passed him I thought I could get away but I quickly realised that in fact I was holding him up. He had more speed than me and it was only a matter of time before I lost the lead.'

Malaysia, Sepang. He qualified second and knew that if he could have put his three best sectors together to make one lap he'd have had pole. In the race he was second – to Ralf. 'At the start, Michael went completely to the right side of the track, which was easily predictable. When we both came to the first corner I

gave him enough room but he had a bit of understeer and touched me. That was it.' Montoya was given a drive-through penalty, which he considered unfair 'because in my opinion I did not cause the collision and this was a normal racing accident. The climb through the field was very exciting, even if I had to do it twice.'

Brazil, Interlagos. 'There's a very Latin atmosphere here, which I obviously enjoy very much.' He took pole and finished the race fifth. At the lights he was away fast but Schumacher emerged from the corkscrew in front of him. Out at the back of the circuit Montoya attacked and Schumacher swerved in front of him to protect the lead. They touched and Montoya had to pit for a new wing while Schumacher continued – unpunished, unlike Montoya in Sepang. Montoya was angry. 'I thought Michael was a fair guy to race with, but definitely not in the way he came into the middle of the track as I was trying to pass. He cut across and ripped off my front wing. And even though I gave him room, I was penalised. If Michael is allowed to race the way we saw in Brazil, then I will race in the same way from now on.'

San Marino, Imola. He was fourth in qualifying, fourth in the race and disappointed because he expected more but had to 'fight with an imbalance on the car.'

Spain, Barcelona. 'It's not one of my favourite tracks, in spite of being quick, but I spend a lot of my leisure time in Spain. I like the country and culture very much, so that makes up for it.' He qualified fourth after switching to the spare car. 'On the last lap I managed to put the best possible lap together. I don't know how it worked, but it definitely did!' He finished the race behind Schumacher despite a problem during his second

pit stop when he was given the signal to go before the crew had finished their work. 'I hit our chief mechanic who was trying to stop me.' He was only slightly hurt.

Austria, A1-Ring. He qualified fourth and finished the race third. Nobody noticed that: it was drowned by the Ferrari decision to slow Barrichello and give the race to Schumacher on the line.

Monaco, Monte Carlo. 'I can't really say I enjoyed my début in Monaco last year. Initially I thought it would be a lot more fun than it was. In fact it was extremely hard work. Racing in Monaco is also a bit strange because the track is 150 yards from my house and I use the "track" all year round, whenever I have to go somewhere. It's a very fancy weekend and a glamorous event but maybe it's a bit too classy and I am not really that kind of person.' He took pole and in the race ran second to Coulthard, keeping Schumacher behind him, then he felt a 'loss of engine power'.

Canada, Montreal. He took pole again – a tremendous lap, riding the kerbs. In the race he ran second and was closing on Schumacher when the Williams expired in smoke.

Europe, Nürburgring. Before he arrived he said: 'A few days have passed since the Canadian Grand Prix and I have finally recovered from the great disappointment.' He took pole yet again, which 'came as a bit of a surprise. After the morning's session we were not expecting anything higher than the second row, actually.' He was running fourth in the race when, with the car undriveable, he retired. 'I couldn't help spinning coming in to the first corner and unfortunately I hit Coulthard, who was close behind me. When I came back to the pits I apologised to him.'

Before the British Grand Prix, Montoya spent a day at Thruxton doing promotional work for BMW. Drivers may regard such days as necessary chores but he was

Familiar sight for Monaco folk, and in 2002 this particular resident looked set to blow everyone out of the water . . . (Getty Images)

Montoya gives his own version of corporate hospitality – using BMW road power – by taking guests round Thruxton at speed. Chris Rea, a motorsport fan, seems tickled not terrified, and Marc Gene has seen all this before. (Bruce Grant-Braham)

The stairway to happiness, 2002. (LAT)

natural, refreshing and enthusiastic. The event gives an insight into Montoya the man – and stands in contrast to the 'seriousness' of Formula 1 mentioned earlier.

As a matter of record, Montoya had driven in three races there: 1995 in Vauxhall and 1996, twice, in Formula 3.

Peter Walker, BMW Special Events manager, organised the promotional day and remembers having to rush off to buy a burger for him 'because he wasn't going to do anything until he'd had a Big Mac or whatever he wanted'. Clearly although Montoya had broadened his culinary demands from the *roast chic-ken! roast chicken!* of 1995, he hadn't broadened them much.

Walker says 'we had an opportunity to use Montoya for promotional purposes, if you like, on one day this year [2002]. We had two objectives, really: to expose some of our best corporate customers to some of our high performance cars and at the same time hopefully give them the most thrilling experience of their lives. Montoya was going to take care of that.

'We invited about 35 customers and they were able to drive a range of these high performance cars

themselves, both on the track and off the track, and then they were given two fast passenger laps either with Montoya or Marc Gene.[2] It was the luck of the draw, in a sense, which driver they got because we knew Montoya wouldn't be able to give everyone a ride. In the evening he came back here to Bracknell[3] and there was an opportunity for all our staff to meet him, get him to sign autographs. Murray Walker interviewed him and we had Patrick Head as well. That was all about staff motivation.

'He really is a super character. He certainly calls a spade a spade and I feel he has such a *strong* personality. You always get some sort of a reaction from him and an audience always reacts to him. He also says exactly what he means. He doesn't hold back: it's that Latin temperament.'

Bruce Grant-Braham, 'involved in motor racing on and off in a variety of situations since 1968' – including taking pictures – was one of the two photographers invited to the event. 'It was one of those days that Juan Pablo has written into his contract to look after his sponsors. They invited fleet buyers along to be wined and dined, and the pinnacle of the day was to have some fast laps round Thruxton in a BMW M5.[4]

'It was an interesting place for them to pick because he won in Formula 3 at Thruxton. It was quite evident that although there were a few years missing between visits he knew his way round extraordinarily well. It took very little time for him to get in the groove.

'I suppose all these people like Montoya have an aura about them. Everyone was eagerly awaiting his arrival – myself included – but we were not quite sure what sort of person he would be. To say we were pleasantly surprised would be an understatement. He turned out to be a true enthusiast. For example he saw this line of BMWs of various types – a full range: sports cars, saloons, about 15 or 20 models – in the pit road and he genuinely wondered if he could leap into each one and try it out. He was really interested in what the handling characteristics were: in how, I suppose, they could be pushed to the limit. The cars were slower than Formula 3 but very potent road cars.

'As an individual he was very easy to chat to and very easy to get to know. OK, he was away from the pressure of hundreds of journalists around and photographers poking their lenses, because they were deliberately excluded. He was totally relaxed. None of us were very sure whether he'd be very fluent in English but he was brilliantly so and could chat to everybody – including Chris Rea[5] who was there amongst the celebrities – very easily about almost anything. He's got a nice, cheeky sense of humour. He's very jolly and he's willing to crack a joke and some of those jokes can be at his own expense. He's very self-effacing, which again was quite a surprise to me having coming up against a few "names" in sport at various times.

'They signalled the M5 saloon as the one they particularly wanted him to drive. It's 0–62 in 5.3 seconds. People were eagerly anticipating their run with him but when they saw him do the first few starts out of the pit road I think some were having second thoughts. The rear tyres were burning doing dragster starts – but that's all part of the skill, I suppose. When you first saw the car at the angles it was at you thought "my God, there's a hooligan behind the wheel" but when it was held in a slide for so long – and being played on the

throttle – you realised he does have a sixth sense, he does have that something special which can hold a vehicle like that, never mind a Formula 1 car.

'He did these fast laps and people were really happy. There were occasions when he was doing doughnuts [rotating the car on its axis] just to show how in control he was. I talked to a lot of people who went with him and there were bits of the circuit where, even in an M5, he was nudging the 120mph mark. People were saying they felt he was going to lose it, the back end was getting loose – but it did come back and they never felt they were imperilled in any way. Apparently he was talking to most people all the time whilst he was doing this.'

Grant-Braham concludes that 'there's a fire in him. If anybody is going to take Michael Schumacher on, he will be the one, given the same or equal machinery. Yes, absolutely. They'd be wheel banging…'

Britain, Silverstone. He took pole although (again) where this lap came from mystified him because the car had been changed so much during the session.

Richard Dutton has a lovely anecdote about Silverstone. Fortec were there, with Renault engines, just outside the Renault Formula 1 pit. 'Who should come along but Montoya. It was our qualifying and he stood for the whole session with us talking about life. We qualified first and second and he really enjoyed it. He could relate to it and it was so nice to spend half an hour talking about old times. He was chilled out, laid back, very calm.

'He hadn't changed – he was the same person the day he walked into our place in 1996, the same lovely, warm guy. A little crazy, but that craziness is fantastic! There's a *sparkle* there.'

Montoya finished third – 'a crazy race because of the changing weather conditions'. He'd run well at the start but when the rain came his Michelin wet tyres were no match for the Bridgestones on the Ferrari.

France, Magny-Cours. He took pole again. 'This was really a good qualifying, probably my best so far.' He struggled with the car in the race and finished fourth while Schumacher took the championship. 'I think it's great for him. He did the best job in the paddock, he has the best car and he knows how to use it.'

Germany, Hockenheim. The circuit had been heavily revised, so was 'a bit of a gamble for everyone'. He qualified fourth and on his last lap 'I made a mistake at the hairpin, I locked the front tyres there'. He inherited second place in the race when Ralf and Barrichello had problems, and this after an 'entertaining' duel with Kimi Räikkönen (McLaren). 'After he passed me at the start I had a few chances to overtake him but it was too risky and I preferred waiting. Then the team told me I could make it and pumped my revs up. Räikkönen made a mistake and I got past.'

Hungary, Budapest. He qualified fourth but couldn't find the right balance for the car and finished the race eleventh. 'Right after the start someone hit me, then I went off on a kerb and lost a piece of bodywork. Due to the ongoing understeer, my left elbow is hurting. From time to time my car was almost impossible to drive.'

I'd asked Helmut Marko how, having run Montoya in Formula 3000, he evaluated his performance in Formula 1.

'A little bit of the old problems: quick when every-

Horseplay at Hockenheim didn't disguise the fact that Montoya was becoming a pain in the neck for the reigning World Champion.
(Getty Images)

thing is fine and the car suits him – fantastic – but if something goes a little bit wrong, like the start at Helsinki for us, he has a very bad race. This time in Hungary showed he has still to learn to calm down more and, even if the car's not working, stay relaxed and think analytically. That is the biggest difference to Michael Schumacher and also the other Schumacher. Ralf analyses everything. For sure he doesn't have the speed of Montoya but sometimes he manages to be faster. As we say, if it's not running right Montoya just *shouts around* instead of concentrating and making the best out of what is not the optimum in terms of the car – which will always happen in racing.'

Belgium, Spa. He qualified fifth after the familiar struggle with the car's balance. He pointed out, however, that he hadn't qualified as low as the third row of the grid since Australia. He got past Räikkönen early on and resisted heavy pressure from Coulthard to finish the race third.

Italy, Monza. His thinking now was to take points from Barrichello and maybe take second place in the championship from him too, before season's end (Barrichello led by seven points going to Monza). The talk was of what BMW's power might deliver. Certainly, it gave him pole. 'We knew we would be at ease on this track from the start.' At ease? As we saw in the Introduction, that BMW engine delivered 19,0000rpm for the first time in history and Montoya's lap was the fastest average speed ever done in a Formula 1 car, 161.449mph (259.819kmh), beating Keke Rosberg who'd done 160.925mph (258.976kmh) at Silverstone, also in a Williams, in 1985. 'I think it's good,' Montoya would say, 'but as long as we keep coming back to Monza and the track doesn't change much, probably next year it is going to be beaten again. It is pretty amazing how quick we went, about two seconds a lap quicker than last year.'

He retired from the race with a suspension problem.

USA, Indianapolis. 'From a technical perspective, the circuit has a lot of rhythm and an important key is a well balanced car.' He qualified fourth ('disappointing

and frustrating') and finished the race fourth. On the second lap Montoya and Ralf crashed, much to the fury of Technical Director Patrick Head, who said it was 'totally unacceptable'.

Montoya's version: 'I was passing Ralf and I braked late. I was going round the outside and suddenly he hit me. I think he braked a lot later.' Ralf's version: 'It is always difficult to pass anyone on the outside. There wasn't a lot of room there at all. Most important is that such things should not happen between team-mates no matter who's responsible.' Head said that both men had to mature: 'Neither of the drivers at the moment are champions. I'm very unimpressed'.[6]

This is as good a place as any to listen to the overall evaluation of David Sears. 'I believe that there are things which require attention, and Frank Williams has identified them as well. Montoya, like Senna, didn't work on his fitness as much as he should have done because he thought his natural talent would carry him all the way. As Frank has categorically said to him: "as far as I am concerned you have to have a fitness trainer, you have to have *this* and you have to have *that* because Schumacher has them and he's the benchmark. So you have got to have a better fitness trainer than him, you've got to train better and so on: then you've got more of a chance of beating him." Originally Senna didn't want to be fit but he realised he *had* to be. I think Montoya, as he wants it more and more, is getting more and more dedicated but realistically he still has a way before he'll rank as a driver with everything complete. He is now starting to realise the bits that are missing – he's still bits to learn – and when he's done that he'll be World Champion.

'When he was in Formula 3 he won one or two races with a Mitsubishi engine, which nobody really liked, and that was pretty bloody good. In 3000, it was obvious his balance was exceptional even on quad bikes in the paddock. He could get them onto two wheels – or even one! – and *still* wave to you. His natural balance and instincts are second to none. The

Balance and
solitude at Spa.
(Getty Images)

rest of it he is now starting to polish up.'

Montoya, Sears feels, is 'much more Latino' than Senna but there is at least one strong similarity. 'You knew that if Senna was nudging your rear wing because you wouldn't let him past, he'd drive through you and sod it. If you both go off, you both go off. Montoya – the same.'

Japan, Suzuka. After his second place in 2001 he approached the weekend with 'reasonable confidence'. He was fourth in free practice and had a 'bad crash which damaged my car quite heavily. I went on the throttle like always and I thought I was going to make the corner fine but instead I went over the sharp part of the kerb and lost the car. The impact was hard.' He qualified a 'disappointing' sixth and finished the race fourth. 'The strategy was bringing the car home and that is what I did.' He was 'delighted' to be third in the Championship. 'It's been a good season and the only regret I have is that I could not get any race victories.'

Perhaps the last word should go to Mo Nunn, because he's been in Formula 1 and CART, and worked so closely with Montoya in 1999 before leaving Ganassi to start his own team.

'I was the man on the radio to him. He was fine. Nothing was ever a problem. He would drive the wheels off the car. I'm not sure now, with Williams, but at that time I would say if you put him in the same car as everybody else, told them *OK, do five laps each* he would be the quickest guy with any kind of car. You took a car – wouldn't matter whose – and put a set-up on it, he would get the most out of it.

'You got 100 per cent every lap he drove. I would never tell him to push. I knew once he reached a certain time, anything more had to come from the car, not him. I would talk to him, get the best out of him and then make a change to the car.' Nunn illustrates the importance of this. 'There's a famous old saying: *if you've got a 200mph car, don't try and do 202*. When you feel in the seat of your pants that the car is ready to get away from you, you'd better stop accelerating because there's nowhere to go.'

The question for Montoya's third season in Formula 1 was: could BMW and Williams give him a car with which to challenge Ferrari? F1 ached for that. The next question was: would he take that car to 2mph beyond? Everyone ached to see that too.

USA Grand Prix
and the
unacceptable face
of racing – team-
mates spinning into
each other.
(Getty Images)

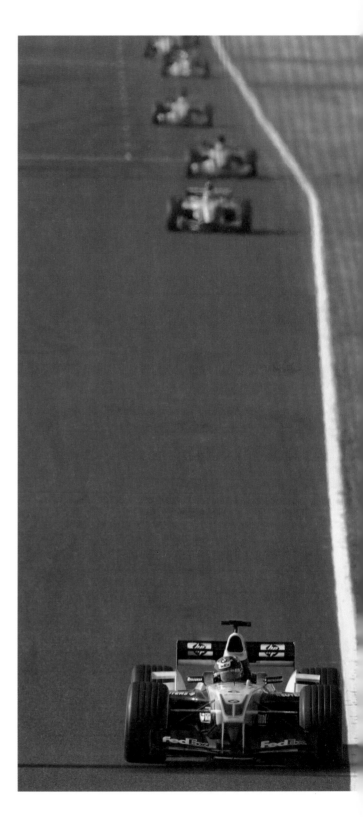

By the end of the
2002 season
this looked to be
the order of
things to come.
(Getty Images)

Nunn has no doubts. 'Montoya will be very good for Formula 1. He'd be good for any series.'

Michael Andretti would agree. 'I think Juan has done an excellent job. As the year went on [in 1999] I was telling everybody "that guy's going to be World Champion one day". He was really special: he could take a car to the limit where he looked like he was crazy. Even on an oval he'd run it almost sideways and everybody was waiting for him to crash. He never did. He has *incredible* car control and I gained a ton of respect for the guy. I think if he is in an equal car he can take Michael Schumacher on. The other thing about Juan is that he's very strong mentally, he doesn't give a crap about what anybody thinks – and that's what you need to be like in Formula 1. I repeat: he has the mental capacity to be World Champion.'

NOTES

1. *Autosport*, 5 April, 2001.
2. Marc Gene, the Williams Number 1 test driver.
3. BMW HQ.
4. A hot BMW, doing 0–100mph in 11.5 seconds.
5. Balladeer and motorsport enthusiast.
6. *Autosport*, 3 October 2002.

statistics

1986
karting
local and national junior champion

1987–1989
karting
Championships in the Kart Komet category

1990
karting
Competed in Junior Worlds, Lonato, Italy

1991
karting
Competed in Junior Worlds, Laval, France

1992
Skip Barber Course USA
Copa Formula Renault
Colombia   8 races   5 poles, 4 wins

1993
National Swift Championship   8 races, 8 poles, 7 wins

1994
Barber Saab – podium finishes only
27 Feb   Miami   FL/1
19 Mar   Sebring   2
13 Aug   Mid-Ohio   P/FL/1

Championship: D. Guzman 128 points,
                   M Hotchkis 122,
                   Montoya 114.

Formula N Mexico   4 poles, 3 wins

1995
Formula Vauxhall
2 Apr   Donington   4
17 Apr   Brands Hatch   DNF
8 May   Thruxton   3
14 May   Silverstone   8
29 May   Oulton Park   2
11 Jun   Brands Hatch   DNF
24 Jun   R 1 Donington   P/1
25 Jun   R 2   2
29 Jul   R 1Knockhill   4
30 Jul   R 2   6
14 Aug   Brands Hatch   3
28 Aug   Snetterton   3
10 Sept   Oulton Park   P/FL/1
24 Sept   Silverstone   P/1

Championship: J Kane 146,
                   M O'Connell 129,
                   Montoya 125.

International Formula 3
22 Oct   Donington   9

Bogotá Six Hours
              Bogotá   Class win

Formula Vauxhall. (LAT)

1996

British Formula 3

31 Mar	R 1 Silverstone	2
	R 2 Silverstone	12
14 Apr	Thruxton	FL/4
5 May	Donington	FL/1
27 May	R 1 Brands Hatch	12
	R 2 Brands Hatch	2
8 Jun	Oulton	FL/9
23 Jun	Donington	FL/13
13 Jul	Silverstone	7
28 Jul	Thruxton	FL/1
11 Aug	Snetterton	3
1 Sept	R 1 Pembrey	4
	R 2 Pembrey	6
29 Sept	R 1 Zandvoort	P/4
	R 2 Zandvoort	DNF
13 Oct	Silverstone	5

Championship: R. Firman 188,
K. Mollekens 148,
J. Kane 146.
5, Montoya 137.

Marlboro Masters

| 4 Aug | Zandvoort | 4 |

Int. Touring Cars

| 18 Aug | R 1 Silverstone | DNF |
| | R 2 Silverstone | DNF |

Non-Championship

| 17 Nov | Macau | R |

Bogotá Six Hours

| | Bogotá | 1 |

1997

Formula 3000

11 May	Silverstone	DNF
19 May	Pau	P/FL/1
5 May	Helsinki	P/DNF
29 Jun	Nürburgring	4
20 Jul	Enna	11
26 Jul	Hockenheim	FL/5
3 Aug	A1-Ring	P/1
23 Aug	Spa	DIS
28 Sept	Mugello	3
25 Oct	Jerez	1

Championship: R. Zonta 39,
Montoya 37.5,
J. Watt 25.

1998

Formula 3000

11 Apr	Oschersleben	P/FL/15
26 Apr	Imola	P/DNF
9 May	Barcelona	P/1
16 May	Silverstone	P/FL/1
23 May	Monaco	FL/6
1 Jun	Pau	P/FL/1
25 Jul	A1-Ring	2
1 Aug	Hockenheim	3
15 Aug	Hungaroring	3
29 Aug	Spa	P/2
6 Sept	Enna	FL/1
26 Sept	Nürburgring	P/3

Championship: Montoya 65,
N Heidfeld 58,
G Rodriguez 33.

1999

FedEx CART series

21 Mar	Miami	10
10 Apr	Motegi (Jap)	13
18 Apr	Long Beach	1
2 May	Nazareth	P/1
15 May	Rio	1
29 May	Madison	P/11
6 Jun	Milwaukee	10
20 Jun	Portland	P/2
27 Jun	Cleveland	P/1
11 Jul	Elkhart Lake	DNF
18 Jul	Toronto	DNF
25 Jul	Michigan	2
8 Aug	Detroit	P/DNF
15 Aug	Mid-Ohio	1
22 Aug	Chicago	1
5 Sept	Vancouver	P/1
12 Sept	Laguna Seca	8
26 Sept	Houston	P/DNF
17 Oct	Surfers Paradise	DNF
31 Oct	Fontana, Calif.	4

Championship: Montoya 212 (most wins tie-break, 7–3).
D. Franchitti 212,
P. Tracy 161.

2000
FedEx CART series

26 Mar	Homestead	DNF
16 Apr	Long Beach	DNF
30 Apr	Rio	DNF
14 May	Motegi	P/7
27 May	Nazareth	P/4
28 May	(Indy 500) Indianapolis	1
4 Jun	Milwaukee	P/1
18 Jun	Detroit	P/DNF
25 Jun	Portland	DNF
2 Jul	Cleveland	6
16 Jul	Toronto	DNF
23 Jul	Michigan	1
30 Jul	Chicago	P/DNF
13 Aug	Lexington	DNF
20 Aug	Elkhart Lake	DNF
3 Sept	Vancouver	DNF
10 Sept	Laguna Seca	6
17 Sept	Gateway, St. Louis	P/1
1 Oct	Houston	2
15 Oct	Surfers Paradise	P/DNF
30 Oct	Fontana	10

Championship: G de Ferran 168,
A Fernandez 158,
R Moreno 147.
9 Montoya, 126.

2001
Formula 1

4 Mar	Australia	DNF
18 Mar	Malaysia	DNF
1 Apr	Brazil	DNF
15 Apr	San Marino	DNF
29 Apr	Spain	2
13 May	Austria	DNF
27 May	Monaco	DNF
10 Jun	Canada	DNF
24 Jun	Europe	FL/2
1 Jul	France	DNF
15 Jul	Britain	4
29 Jul	Germany	P/FL/DNF
19 Aug	Hungary	8
2 Sept	Belgium	P/DNF
16 Sept	Italy	P/1
30 Sept	USA	FL/DNF
14 Oct	Japan	2

Championship: M Schumacher 123,
D Coulthard 65,
R Barrichello 56.
6 Montoya, 31.

2002
Formula 1

3 Mar	Australia	2
17 Mar	Malaysia	FL/2
31 Mar	Brazil	P/FL/5
14 Apr	San Marino	4
28 Apr	Spain	2
12 May	Austria	3
26 May	Monaco	P/DNF
9 Jun	Canada	P/FL/DNF
23 Jun	Europe	P/DNF
7 Jul	Britain	P/3
21 Jul	France	P/4
28 Jul	Germany	2
18 Aug	Hungary	11
1 Sept	Belgium	3
15 Sept	Italy	P/DNF
29 Sept	USA	4
13 Oct	Japan	4

Championship: M Schumacher 144,
Barrichello 77,
Montoya 50.

Pole at Monaco in 2002,
first of five in a row.
(Getty Images)

index